A PLUME BOOK

PITTSBURGH DAD

CHRIS PREKSTA (director/cocreator) is a film and web series director whose credits include *Pittsburgh Dad*, the sci-fi series *The Mercury Men*, which premiered on the NBC Universal/ Syfy digital network, and the award-winning online sitcom *The Guild*. Chris grew up in Pittsburgh, Pennsylvania.

CURT WOOTTON (Pittsburgh Dad/cocreator), a film and stage actor, turned an impression of his actual father into a nationally known character with the introduction of *Pittsburgh Dad*. His credits also include the online series *Captain Blasto* and *The Mercury Men*. Curt grew up in Greensburg, Pennsylvania.

Chris and Curt are currently writing and developing *Pittsburgh Dad* as a feature film.

www.youtube.com/pittsburghdad
www.pghdad.com

Pittsburgh Dad

Everything Your Dad Has Said to You

Chris Preksta
and Curt Wootton

A PLUME BOOK

PLUME
Published by the Penguin Group
Penguin Group (USA) LLC
375 Hudson Street
New York, New York 10014

USA | Canada | UK | Ireland | Australia
New Zealand | India | South Africa | China
penguin.com
A Penguin Random House Company

First published by Plume, a member of Penguin Group (USA) LLC, 2015

Photographs by Chris Preksta

 REGISTERED TRADEMARK—MARCA REGISTRADA

LIBRARY OF CONGRESS CATALOGING-IN-PUBLICATION DATA
Preksta, Chris.
Pittsburgh dad : everything your dad has said to you / Chris Preksta, Curt Wootton.
pages cm
ISBN 978-0-14-218172-0 (paperback)
I. Wootton, Curt. II. Pittsburgh dad (Internet television program) III. Title.
PN1992.77.P46P84 2015
791.45'72—dc23
2014039840

Printed in the United States of America
5 7 9 10 8 6 4

Set in Janson Text LT Std
Designed by Leonard Telesca

To our parents,
for raising us right and giving us
endless material along the way

Acknowledgments

Thank you to:

Curt's girlfriend, Kaitlin, for putting up with being called "Deb."

Chris's wife, Ashley, for her endless support of a nerdy husband. Jane and Catherine, for making Chris an actual Pittsburgh Dad.

Linda and Dave Urbaniak, for allowing their actual home to become a TV studio once a week.

Randy Baumann, Bill Crawford, and Sally Wiggin, for graciously helping our audience to grow larger than just our families.

Nicholas Yon and Turner's Dairy for their consistent partnership.

Coach Mike Tomlin and the Pittsburgh Steelers for allowing us to be a part of the family.

Editor Becky Cole for guiding two first-time authors.

George Ruiz and David Sedelmeier for working to make sure we can both create AND pay our bills.

All the fans, for watching and sharing their own memories with us over the years. Without them, you'd be holding a blank book.

The city of Pittsburgh, for being the best city on the planet.

Introduction

"OH MY GOSH, IT'S MY FATHER!"

In October 2011, just to kill some time one afternoon, we decided to film Curt doing an impression of his often-cranky father, complete with his thick Pittsburgh accent (down is pronounced "dahn," house = "hahs," for those of yinz who've never heard it). We grabbed some old glasses from a thrift store and quickly shot a forty-second video on Chris's iPhone:

"Did yinz warsh your feet off in that little bucket by the pool ladder before yinz got in that pool? I don't want grass clippings clogging up my filter. And no I ain't turning on the air-conditioning, I got fans blowing. Just go get some freeze pops in the cellar."

We added an *All in the Family*–style sitcom intro and fake studio laughter to make it appear as if Curt's father was a TV dad from the '70s or '80s. We were just doing it to make our own parents laugh. When we uploaded the video "Meet Pittsburgh Dad" onto YouTube to share with our families, we expected a total of 50 views. That first day, we had 1,000. Within just a few months, we had more than 1 million views. National news outlets began sharing the episode, and we were flooded with hundreds of messages and comments from around the country all saying similar things: "My dad is EXACTLY like this!" "It's scary how accurate this is." "It's as if you secretly recorded my family growing up!"

It seemed like everybody's parents said the same things to them when they were growing up. Was there some class that taught all dads to yell about not pressing your face against the screen door? Do you automatically start guarding the thermostat the moment you become a parent? At what age do we suddenly start regulating how much milk is poured into a cereal bowl?

Over the past three years, that single video has led to more than 100 additional episodes capturing the nostalgia, funny phrases, and frustrations of growing up in a blue-collar, middle-class home—coming home when the street lights go on, catching lightning bugs, and not being allowed to play in the "good" living room.

What you're holding is a collection of our favorite jokes and stories written for the show, collected from our personal experiences and memories of growing up. But you'll swear it was your own dad speaking.

And if you picked up this book wondering what the hell it is, or why you should care about some dad from Pittsburgh, you can see the show for yourself at **www.youtube.com/ pittsburghdad**. Millions of views later, we still film on Chris's iPhone.

We hope yinz enjoy it!

EATING FAMILY DINNER

The food tastes the same in all the chairs. Warsh your hands and sit the hell down!

Can you have a Happy Meal?! You should just be *happy* you're even getting *this* meal.

Can we eat dinner at IKEA tonight?! Why don't we grab hors d'oeuvres down at Roomful Express while we're at it?

What's city chicken?! It's pork. If you don't like it, just close your eyes and pretend it's chicken nuggets.

Jessica, I rinsed the apple off. It's clean, for crying out loud. You won't eat fruit until we soak it in Purell and run it through the dishwasher.

Take that wrapped Arby's sandwich outta the microwave before you blow up my house!

Hey, what's the number-one rule in the house? "Always use a Chip Clip."

Quit eating all the Little Debbie snacks! Those are for your lunches.

No, I don't want no craft beer. I don't even like their mac and cheese.

PICKY EATERS

You have to eat it 'cause there's kids starving in China. Send it to them, then?! How's about we just send you, instead?

You're a vegetarian? Since when did Cinnamon Toast Crunch become a vegetable?

No, this ain't like eating in a prison. They complain less there.

Quit feeding the animals under the table. That dog eats better than some families I know.

Hey, Mum, stop throwing all that leftover bread to them filthy birds. It's starting to look like a damn Hitchcock movie out there.

Can we make you something else?! Sorry you ain't happy with tonight's selection at Mom's Diner. Let's see what else we have on the menu. Oh look, a hot plate of *nothing* with a delicious side of *grounded*.

Whaddya mean Dr. Oz says we should use sea salt instead? Since when are we taking health advice from a wizard? Is Dr. Oz gonna pay our grocery bill?

Them rumors about Mountain Dew ain't true! I used to drink it all the time and here are you three goofs complaining.

GOING SHOPPING

I found this *Sopranos* DVD box set in the five-dollar bin, so all I'm paying is five dollars. If it got in there by mistake, that sounds like a Walmart problem.

Wait in line for hours to see the "Cake Boss"?! Yeah, Deb, I'd love to explain that to my *real* boss.

Nah, Mum will have to take yinz shopping down that Hollister's. You need a lantern and a map to shop at that place.

Yeah, Mum "bought" yinz book covers. They're in the kitchen and say Giant Eagle on them.

You have a dime. Quit asking the penny-candy lady about your Swedish Fish and Flying Saucer "options" like you're buying a new SUV.

Where's Gram? Over there talking to the self-checkout machine.

No, we ain't buying yinz Lunchables. There's bread and chipped ham in the fridge. I don't care if only the ends are left, them are just as good. And quit eating all the Pepperidge Farm cookies. Those are adult cookies.

GIVING RIDES TO THE MOVIES

No, I ain't ridin' yinz to the movies. It's raining, it's slippy out there. We are in for the night. And don't bother asking Mum, 'cause she has night blindness. She'll end up over an embankment 'cause yinz had to see *Gravity*? She's gonna *feel* gravity when that car rolls down a hill.

Do yinz see a Yellow Cab Company sign on the front of the house? I'm gonna put a little light on my head that says "OFF DUTY."

High time yinz start buying tickets for the Shoelace Express.

I don't care if Erin's mom drives her places. That's just 'cause she watches too much *Unsolved Mysteries*. Thinks everyone's out to kidnap her daughter. I seen that woman drive Erin fifty feet from the bus stop to the house. Might as well pull up right next to the bus and have Erin jump out, like in *Speed*.

You wanna see a movie, yinz can go down the cellar and watch them *Titanic* VHS tapes. Whaddya mean the first tape is missing?! Good. Now you get right to the good parts, all the people falling and hitting the propeller.

You can't use the big TV 'cause Mum's in there watching *The Good Wife*. And I'm in here trying to hide from the Loud Wife and the Expensive Wife.

No, if yinz wanna see *Dawn of the Planet of the Apes*, just go watch your uncle Rick try to install his wireless router.

No, we ain't ordering movies "on demand." Them charges appear *on* my bill. Now move *on* with your lives 'cause you're getting *on* my nerves.

What can you do at the mall that you can't do here? Hey, yinz can play in that refrigerator box in the cellar. Pretend that's the mall. Then pretend you're the garbage men and throw it out.

Pap ain't driving yinz. He don't know where the hell he's going anymore. You'll end up in a real rough part of town like in *Judgment Night*. And Emilio Estevez won't be there to help ya.

No, Uncle Rick's car ain't safe. Got parts on it from twenty other cars. Only place that car can take yinz to is Thunderdome. That car drives by, I half expect to see it being chased by Terminators.

There ain't no way Jeffy's mum has clean-enough breath at this hour to get her car started.

SLUMBER PARTIES

What do yinz got, *three* Ouija boards?! Geez, next I'm gonna have to get a priest to come to the house.

Light as a feather, stiff as a board? Well, Brittany can't weigh more than sixty-two pounds anyhows.

No, Bloody Mary don't appear when you say her name three times. Only place you're gonna find Bloody Mary is in my breakfast tomorrow morning.

What is it with you girls and these devil games? The first thing you do when all you little girls get together is seek out the devil.

No, Dana ain't a witch. She plays softball. Her dad works down H&R Block.

Geez, how many bottles of nail polish you girls got going right now?! I half expected the carbon monoxide detector to go off. Just nobody light a match. And I don't want any of that nail-polish remover on that coffee table. That'll take the stain right off of it.

Don't just bite right into them pizza rolls. They just came outta the oven. That's like lava in there.

And who the hell are you all texting? You're all in the same room together! Better not be any of them mean texts like I heard about on *20/20*.

Yinz are playing Truth or Dare? Well, the *truth* is I gotta get up early tomorrow so don't *dare* wake me up with any noise tonight.

You're playing Clue, huh? Well, let me tell ya how it ends. Yinz killed *Dad*, in the *living room*, with the *noise*!

PLAYING BOARD GAMES

How old is this Scrabble game? What are the letters carved out of, elephant tusks? Had *y* and *z* even been invented yet?

No, we can't play Twister since yinz used it as a picnic blanket last summer and never put it away.

Before we play Trivial Pursuit, we have to play "try and get the pie piece out with a butter knife."

How do you play Mouse Trap?! Step one: Set up the trap. Step two: Let it go one time. Step three: Throw the game right into a garage sale.

Yinz wanna play Family Feud? Does it come with Richard Dawson's flask? Geez, even the board smells like bourbon and polyester. I swear that guy got a couple girls pregnant in the middle of an episode.

Deb, I think it's time to get a new Jeopardy game. 'Cause Alex Trebek ain't had a mustache in twenty years and half the answers are Princess Di; Pan Am; and Luke and Laura.

We lost the Operation pincers, so go get Mum's eyebrow tweezers. This Operation guy don't got the funny bone or the gumband no more. He don't need us. He needs Dr. Kevorkian.

Why can't we play Mastermind? Well, for starters, you ate a couple of the pieces when you were little, so I'm not sure you qualify for this game.

No, we ain't playing Dungeons & Dragons, 'cause that leads to the devil. Remember when that Paul kid started sleepwalking? Dungeons & Dragons. And Derek Englert bought that big snake? Dungeons & Dragons.

Yinz lost all the marbles? Well then, looks like we're playing Starving, Starving Hippos.

PLAYING MONOPOLY

Monopoly? Geez, we got a couple weeks on our hands? Yinz still ain't finished that one you got going over Gram's house. When you started that game, *Great*-Grandma was still alive.

I'm the racecar, Mum is the iron, and Brandon you're gonna have to be a battery from outta the junk drawer. Go get it.

No, Brandon, you ain't being the banker. You lost that job after you spent all sixty-five dollars of your birthday money to try and get the watch out of the claw game.

Well, unless there's a "beg Dad for twenty dollars" card under Community Chest, you just lost Baltic Avenue. Don't cry about it, 'cause I own Water Works, too.

Yinz two keep fighting and you can go to your room, do not pass Go, do not collect two hundred dollars!

PLAYING WITH LEGO

Brandon, that LEGO is two hundred dollars! For two hundred bucks I can get you four pallets of *real* bricks down Home Depot. Couldn't get you to help me build a retaining wall, but throw a couple plastic bricks your way and suddenly you're Frank Lloyd Wright.

What do you even need more pieces for, Brandon? You

turn every piece into a laser gun anyhows. Antenna, it's a gun. Little bullhorn, it's a gun. Coffee mug, it's a gun.

Can you imagine PennDOT building LEGOs? It would take them three months just to snap on one piece. Step one: Open the box. Step two: Stand around and look at the pieces for three years.

When I was a kid, I didn't have LEGOs. I had Playmobil. My grandma bought them down the Christian shop. They come over from East Germany. There weren't no creativity with them toys. If you got a gas station, it had to be a gas station. Have fun playing with the Playmobil Municipal Building. Only accessories it had was W2 forms. Playmobil don't come with instructions, it comes with rules. They even warned ya right on the box not to interact with any other toys.

PLAYING VIDEO GAMES

What the hell are yinz playing? Grand Theft Auto?! All I hear is gunshots, sirens, and women screaming. Does this video game take place at Ray Lewis's house?

Did Mum see yinz playing this game? She don't even like you jumping on them Mario turtles; she sure as hell ain't gonna like you stealing that old woman's car and running her over with it.

Who bought you this game anyhows? Grandma?! She don't even know what the hell she's buying anymore.

This is just like the time yinz talked her into taking you to see that *Django Unchained* because you told her it was about a bear escaping the circus.

Can you borrow the credit card to buy a hat for your Xbox avatar?! Brandon, you're lucky we buy you *real* clothes.

THE ATARI

You know what yinz should play? The Atari. Is it made of wood?! Sorta. It was built in the '70s. Game systems back then were like furniture. I think there's even a liquor cabinet built into it.

No, you can't watch Netflix on the Atari. Could you play online with your friends?! Yeah, you got the telephone, you called them up and told them to come over.

Look, we got the E.T. game. Does he have a gun?! When the hell did you see E.T. with a gun? No, you make his head go up and down.

What do you mean, "hit another button"? There's *one* button. You can hit the button or not hit the button. Them's the choices.

GOING TO CHUCK E. CHEESE

Loud kids and snotty noses. This place is one giant flu factory. How many skee-ball tickets is it for a bottle of Airborne?

Good job, Jeffy. It only cost you four hundred dollars to win enough Chuck E. Cheese tickets to get that ten-dollar stuffed animal.

All right, Brandon, that's it for Chuck E. Cheese's. Let's go. And don't go hiding yourself in the ball pit like you're the Predator.

BIRTHDAY CAKE

No, the kids ain't lighting the candles. I told you if you play with fire, you'll pee the bed. Yes, it is too true, Linda. Mr. Wizard talked about it once.

Deb, you don't get bad luck if you don't cut the first piece of your birthday cake. Last week she's throwing salt over her shoulder for good luck. It didn't work, 'cause the next day we had no salt for the potatoes.

ON DAD'S BIRTHDAY

It's my birthday, I choose what we eat, and I want Aunt Linda's stuffed peppers. If it were your birthday, I'd be stuck down Long John Silver's. Sweating all night. That place is a day-ender.

The big birthday treat when I was a kid was Pap would take you down to Children's Palace and let you walk around. Wouldn't get you nothing, but you could look all you want.

What did I wish for? Go in the other room and see if Jeffy is still tapping on my fish tank. He is? Well, I didn't get it.

Do kids get presents on *my* birthday?! If it were up to you kids, we'd be giving you presents on Martin Luther King Jr. Day!

Thanks, Rick: a gift card to Miami Subs. Where the hell is there a Miami Subs around here?

What's this, Linda, a subscription to *People* magazine? I get one month and then I gotta pay the rest of the year? What are you getting me for Christmas, an electric bill?

What'd Jessica get me? She used newspaper instead of wasting good money on wrapping paper. This is a birthday gift in itself.

Mandy already gave me a birthday gift. A cell-phone bill when she didn't go over her minutes.

DOING CHORES

No one wants to change that litter box? Well, then I'm sure the pound won't mind doing it.

When the garbage can is full, you take it out. You don't just stack stuff on top like it's Jenga. And what's this stuff lying around the garbage? What do you think this is, horseshoes?

You're the only kids I know that will carry garbage up to the little garbage can in the bathroom instead of taking the bag out. That one up there is just for Kleenexes and Dixie Cups.

Boy, you kids run away from chores like they was live grenades. Well, if it was fun it wouldn't be called work. *Pay* you?! You're lucky I don't charge yinz room and board. Shame they don't pay people to leave socks lying around the house, 'cause you kids would be millionaires.

Quit leaving your wet towels in the corner of the bathroom. That's how you get earwigs. And when you're done in the shower, wipe them walls down. Mold is growin' in them cracks and it's starting to look like a swamp. Every time I pull back the shower curtain, I half expect the Legion of Doom's headquarters to rise outta the tub.

Mandy, cleaning the family room don't just mean straightening up the magazines on the coffee table. You can still run the sweeper even though its headlight is burned out. You're sweeping the family room not Noah's Ark!

Jessica, your idea of cleaning up is throwing a blanket on the back of the couch and lighting a candle.

No, this ain't child abuse. They ain't gonna lock me up. Next to thieves and killers, the jail's gonna have the dad who made his kids bring the laundry upstairs?

From now on, when I open a DVD case, the right DVD better be in there. Went to watch *Iron Eagle* the other day and I found an America's Online disc in its place.

Look at that microwave. I swear yinz put a gallon of SpaghettiOs in there, revved it up to full power, and walked away. Now everything you heat up tastes like SpaghettiOs.

All done? OK, now get outside and blow the stink off ya.

DOING THE LAUNDRY

Deb, you use too many dryer sheets. I'm pulling them outta my clothes all day like I'm some kind of Snuggles magician!

WATCHING THE SUPER BOWL

The Super Bowl? If the Steelers ain't in it, I'd rather just watch the *Full House* episode of them watching the Super Bowl. And why are all these Steelers cheering for the Ravens in the Super Bowl?! That's like Bambi's mum cheering for the gun.

Who's the half-time show? Bruno Mars?! I'd rather see Bruno Sammartino.

THE OLYMPICS

You kids are gonna be in the Olympics someday? Well, we sure as hell know it won't be curling, 'cause that would mean pickin' up a broom.

PRESIDENT'S DAY

Them kids are celebrating the holiday by removing as many presidents as they can from my wallet.

VALENTINE'S DAY

Would you like some wine, Deb? Don't worry I got a whole box. It's that Pink Zinfandel you like. Is this the kind that's supposed to be warm or cold? 'Cause it's been sitting in the car.

Deb, you look stunning tonight. As radiant as that time when we was at Dairy Queen. And how's 'bout these flowers? The guy told me they last longer if you put aspirin in the vase, but we didn't have none so's I just used Advil.

I got salads chillin' in the fridge and some coleslaw I picked up from down Long John Silver's. And yes, I used a coupon from the Entertainment Book. I was gonna take you down TGI Fridays 'cause they got them potato skins you like, but they sell them in stores now.

I got you a teddy bear. Aw, it's supposed to talk and say, "To My Beary Best Valentine" or something! That's a piece of junk. That's gotta go back to KMart's. I got the receipt in my sock drawer, so's if you're going down there this week, you mind?

I bought you a bottle of that Sarah Parker's Jessica scent you like. You know they wanted fifty dollars down at Macy's for this itty-bitty bottle? I found the same thing over at Burlington's for ten dollars cheaper. That woman at Macy's tried talking me into Sarah Parker's lotions, foot creams, and tote bags. I was half expecting her to hand me Sarah Parker's phone bill.

Deb, I saved you a whole DVR of them *Dance Moms*, the *Teen Moms*, them nutball Kardashians. The clicker is yours. You know, Deb, your real present is upstairs in our bedroom. I put up them curtains that you wanted. Foreplay?! Well, I washed the dishes.

DAUGHTER'S FIRST DATE

Where do you think you're going, young lady? Get the hell outta here, you ain't going on no date. You're fourteen years old. You still got Rainbow Brite curtains in your room.

Well, who's this boy? Andrew who? He related to them Rafalskis over in Turtle Crick? He ain't one of them boys who got caught lighting fireworks behind the school last month, is he? What's his dad do? Is this kid a troublemaker? What kind of grades he get? I can look it up on the Internet if I have to.

Does he play baseball? Does he lift weights? Well, what the hell does he do, then? Skateboards?! Skateboards where? Not down the church; they banned that there!

Well, what's he want to do with his life? Play music?! What kind of music? None of that rap garbage, I hope.

And what are you standing by the door for? That looks like you're doing something secret. I want him to come through that front door and say hi to the whole family.

Where the hell you going, anyways? What movie? Better not be rated R. If you're going to see that *Howard Trains a Dragon 2*, you're taking your little brother with you.

Who's driving you? Well, how long has his brother had his license? Make sure he knows about black ice. 'Cause you can't see it. You don't know it's coming until the car's flipped over the guardrail. And then I don't know nothing about it till the fire whistle goes off.

Tell you what, I'll drive yinz down and pick you up right after. Well, then you ain't going. Pout all you want. I won't lose sleep over it.

ON THE COMPUTER

What did you kids do to the computer, 'cause now it won't print? And who messed up the Internet? Well, how do I install Google? I got three anti-virus programs running and that still ain't enough.

You kids better not be downloading no music. I ain't trying to get sued by that "Jay See."

We bought this computer so's I could pay bills, e-mail your uncle in Florida, and watch the cat-riding-the-sweeper video.

No, don't "send an error report." That goes straight to the

government. I don't need them knowing what we're doing wrong. First, you send an error report; next thing, the SWAT team is kicking down our door.

You kids have been inside all weekend downloading and uploading. When them bills come, I'm gonna be *unloading* on yinz!

If you kids got time to Twitter, then you got time to help me replace the window screens.

FACEBOOK

What do I need Facebook for? So people can tell me I shouldn't eat at Chick-fil-A?

Facebook: a place for friends. Or if you're a woman in my family: a place for neb-shits.

OK, I'm signing up for Facebook. This thing ain't using my credit card, is it? No, I don't need no profile pic. All my friends know what the hell I look like.

What do I gotta type in here? Things I like? OK. . . Ponderosa . . . Steelers . . . Kielbasa.

You can check people into places? OK. They got the orphanage on here?

All this thing is, is babies, cats, and food. People should

post useful stuff, like letting me know when the Shamrock Shake is back.

No, Rick, I ain't building no farm on Facebook. You do more fake work on here than actual work.

Yeah, Linda, everyone wants to see what music you're listening to. Every album you got starts with "Wilson" and ends with "Phillips."

How do I block Tom on this thing? Matter of fact, how do I just block all of Baltimore?

Brandon, what are you doing on here? You're eight years old. What are your "likes"? Mud, Nintendo, and Kool-Aid Jammers.

Can you type the F-word on this? Oh, look, you can! Hey Deb, did you know you could type the F-word on this?! I typed in the F-word and the D-word and the S-word, and it allowed it!

Mandy, I thought you broke up with Andrew. Well, that ain't what your Facebook says. Oh, "it's complicated." You're fourteen years old; what the hell's so complicated? You two act like you're Billy Joel and Christie Brinkley.

Mandy, you were not born in 1988! Don't be pretending you're an adult on here. 'Cause you know what's next, right?

Predators! And not the good kind with heat vision. It's them weirdos that hang out down 7-Eleven and drive white vans with no windows.

Our church is on here? I'm not sure if Jesus would like that. Oh wait, it says he did like it.

How do I share this funny video? Or is that an extra charge?

"Tish just checked in to Dee's Bar." What else is new? It'd be bigger news if she ever checked out of that place.

Mandy's crying because Brittany got more "likes" on her ice-bucket video?! You gotta be kidding me. Well, tell Mandy if she don't get up for school on time tomorrow, she's gonna be waking up to another ice-bucket challenge whether she likes it or not.

Mandy's obsessed with them Facebook "likes." Where's she get it from? Need I remind you, Deb, of the time you got all worked up 'cause June Boyers got over a hundred likes on her "throwing back Thursdays" picture? I'm pretty sure June Boyers buys her likes on Facebook. Three hundred and fifty-seven likes for a lasagna she made is a tad suspicious. It said "Stouffer's" right on the pan. Four hundred and twenty-two likes 'cause she's on Shakeology? You don't see me whining over the eight lousy likes I got after for that nice picture of our tomater plant. But post about a dog taking a nap, geez, open the floodgates: a thousand likes.

Pete's grandma died, he got twenty-two likes. Who the hell likes a dead grandma?!

Sure enough, every time I see a swimsuit video come through the feed, "Uncle Rick liked this." Rick, you know you can just like that in your mind, right? You don't gotta "like it" like it.

What's everyone gonna do with these likes, anyhows? Can you pay the electric bill with likes? Here you go, Duquesne Light: forty-three likes, how's that?

LOOKING THINGS UP

What's Google's phone number? I'm just gonna call them and have them look this up for me.

GOOGLE GLASS

Why the hell would I need Google glasses with GPS? You know what else shows you where you're going when you look through them? Normal glasses!

WATCHING THE ACADEMY AWARDS

Who cares who wins the Oscars anyhows? They only give them to those weirdo movies. *The Last Emperor* ain't on my DVD shelf. You know what is? *Innerspace*! And how did *The Empire Strikes Back* not win best movie?! I notice Spike TV don't show no *Ghandi* marathons around the holidays. Back in '77, you didn't see kids running around with *Annie Hall* action figures and bedsheets. *Shakespeare in Love*? I'd rather see Shakespeare in the ring . . . fighting Mr. T. Netflix recommends that I watch *The King's Speech*? Well, I recommend that they don't bill me no more. I don't think either of us is gonna win. You know what shoulda won an Oscar? *Cannonball Run*! Got Burt Reynolds and Dom DeLuise in a car race across the country against Dean Martin, Jackie Chan, and Terry Bradshaw. But they give the Oscar to *Chariots of Fire*, a whole movie about two nerds jogging.

BEST LEAD ACTRESS IN A DRAMA

And the Oscar for "Best Fit Thrown" goes to my daughter Mandy. Your award is up in your room; get going.

THE WOLF OF WALL STREET

Wolf on Wall Street? Pass. There weren't one wolf in the movie! I waited that entire movie for a full moon to come out and transform that Leonardo DiCappalero, but he just stayed a jag-off the whole time. It's just like that time I got hosed into watching *The Devil Wears Prada*. There weren't no hero fighting Satan, no exorcisms, and no one breathed any fire. Kept waiting for that Anne Castaway to get possessed, and all she did was get yelled at by that Meryl Street.

CAPTAIN PHILLIPS

Captain Phillips was a great idea, but instead of Tom Hanks they should've got Charles Bronson. Trust me, them pirates wouldn't have gotten within a hundred yards of that boat.

AT THE CHURCH FISH FRY

No, Jessica, this does not count as CCD.

What do you mean they *ran* out of cole slaw? How's about I just *run* out of money when that collection plate comes 'round?

Hey, Sister Janice, eight bucks for this little fish sandwich? What is this, a *goldfish* fry?

Why is Father holding them baskets? He better just be collecting beer money. I swear, this church sees a couple people just standing around, they start passing baskets.

Hey, Brandon, don't eat that Slim Jim. There's some kind of meat in them. What'd I tell you? You eat meat on a Friday and you might go to hell. Or worse yet, I'll take them video games away.

Does the bake sale take debit cards?! Yeah, Sister Theresa is up there charging twenty-five-cent brownies to PayPal. What, are you trying to earn SkyMiles?

Geez, if you wanna can of pop, you gotta buy a ticket; she gives it to the guy, he runs it up to Tim's mum, then he brings it down. It's an assembly line for a can of Mountain Dew.

Put them Micro Machines back! I told ya to quit nebbing through the Catholic school kids' desks.

Where did yinz find a *Cheers* coloring book? Geez, this place don't throw nothing out. Well, is it Rebecca or Diane?

Uncle Rick's coming? Geez, I don't even think Sea World has enough fish to fry up for that guy.

Hey, Andrew, take your ball cap off. 'Cause God don't like hats and I don't like the Yankees.

Deb, what do you mean you signed us up to work next week's fish fry? Well, that counts as church, then.

Linda, you were gonna be a nun? Well, that went right out the door when you was caught rolling around with Ron Shumacher in the back of Pizza Hut.

EASTER

Brandon, quit knocking kids over! It's an Easter-egg hunt, not *The Hungry Games*.

The Easter Bunny didn't have no more of that plastic grass left, so he had to use our hamster bedding in your baskets.

No, the Easter Bunny don't give out Xboxes, bikes, or LEGO sets. Keep asking and all he's giving out are smacks, chores, and groundings. He'll even hide them around the house for yinz to find. The Easter Bunny does candy, he don't know nothing about PlayStation games!

CHURCH ATTIRE

I told you to put a shirt on with a collar. Or your Steelers jersey.

AT CHURCH

No, we ain't sitting up front. What's there to see? God's everywhere in here.

What do you mean we can't leave after communion? I

wanna beat the crowds to Eat'n Park. Father can't even see the Gospel; how's he gonna see us leavin' way back here?

Geez, is Father going for the Guinness Record for longest homily of all time? I tell you what, Father's got two minutes to wrap this up, or startin' next week, we're Presbyterian.

If white smoke means they picked a new pope, Uncle Rick's Bonneville has been picking popes for years.

CHURCH BEHAVIOR

Hey, kneel all the way, butt off the pew. I know it hurts; it's supposed to hurt! Quit doodling in them hymnals. And put that kneeler up. You want all the old people in the pew tripping and falling over? Shhh . . . quit giggling over there. There's nothing funny about this place.

No, you already went to the bathroom. Yinz are just jerking around out there. Quit giving your sister Indian burns! Keep it up, you'll be going to CCD five nights a week. No, you ain't playing your video-game thing. You wanna get struck down by lightning? Remember, if you get grounded in here it's worth double.

CHURCH COLLECTION

How many collection plates are they going to pass? Aw, they been raising money for that new air conditioner for five years. I swear, even PBS asks for less money than this place. You see that water damage on that roof? Well, better throw around another collection plate.

GOING TO GRAM'S HOUSE

C'mon, we're going to Gram's house. I don't care if you're in the middle of fighting Mike Tyson's Punch-Out!!, you're going. Grandparents ain't around forever. No, we're not stopping at McDonald's. Aunt Linda's making stuffed peppers for dinner. I don't care if you don't like it, you'll eat it or starve.

What do you mean it stinks over there? Couldn't stink any worse than that room of yours.

I know Pap's eye looks creepy. Just don't look at it.

No, Gram don't got a computer yet. She still has a rotary phone. What the hell's she gonna do with a computer . . . Facebook?

There's plenty of things to do at Gram's house. Your cousins will be there, there's a dart board in the cellar, them Beach Boys records, or yinz can hook up the old Atari. Or yinz can play with that weirdo kid Paul from next door. Just don't touch Pap's pool table.

You guys always have fun over there. Last time you were at Gram's, yinz were sliding down the steps on couch cushions. That's fun! You can't do that here. I'd tear your heads off. Well then, yinz can stare out the window all day for all I care!

No, I don't know if Gram's got gifts for you. That ain't the reason you go visit people. That kind of attitude reflects badly on your mother and me. Get ready; you're going!

AT GRAM'S HOUSE

Hey, Jessica, do me a favor and walk down the little store and buy Grandma some cigarettes. You tell them I said it's OK.

Hey, Rick, do you gotta watch *Game of Thrones* while the kids are playing in there? Don't need a bunch of ten-year-olds seeing naked women on dragons while they're playing Monopoly.

Hey, kids, don't be petting Gram's dog, 'cause it don't like being touched and it hates kids. No, you ain't walking to the mall from her house. I don't know what it is about Gram's place that turns you kids into wandering nomads.

Gram don't got no more hard candy left. Just eat some of them Halls cough drops.

Aw, Deb, I sure hope you didn't throw away that bacon grease sitting by the stove. Gram was saving that to cook with later.

Hey, quit throwing them lawn darts at each other! I don't care if you're playing *The Hungry Games*, you're gonna end up in the hospital. Why don't yinz go out in the street and play something?

Quit ringing Gram's wind chimes like they're the Long John Silver's bell! We ain't got "crunchies," we got groundings.

BASEMENT POP

Hey, you kids better stop drinking all the little cans of ginger ale; those are for adult drinks!

And which one of yinz put a can in the freezer and left it to explode all over? No, I ain't buying no more pop. Yinz only drink half a can and then you leave them lying around the house so's bees and bugs get in them. Oh, don't tell me there ain't nothin' to drink. There's a pitcher of lemon Blennd and Mum bought yinz a whole case of them Little Hug drinks. Keep it up and you'll get nothing but hose water. Boy, I tell ya, you kids don't know how easy you got it. Your biggest struggle in life is getting a straw into a Capri Sun.

THE HOUSE PHONE

Hello? Deb is downstairs. Just call back and I won't answer.

When you kids answer the phone and it's for me, come down and tell me! Don't just stomp your foot three times.

What'd I tell yinz about using that America's Online? I'm sick of picking up the phone and hearing that sound. It sounds like Robocop dying or C-3PO coughing. That's ear torture. It's like *A Clockwork Orange*; put this on that guy's ear for two hours.

It's a rotary phone; there ain't no backspace. You just gotta dial it again. It'd be faster just to walk to your friend's house.

If you're using the phone in the kitchen, stay in the kitchen. You don't walk the phone into the living room and stretch the cord out. I don't know where the cordless is. Did it go down the couch? Try paging it. Hey, Mandy, what are you doing with the cordless across the street?! Bring that back to the house!

I swear, all this phone ever does is ring. You'd think we were running a PBS telethon.

What you doing calling me on my cell phone, it ain't past seven o'clock. You call the house phone.

THE GOOD LIVING ROOM

Hey, which one of yinz was jerking around in the good living room?! The cushions are all messed up like yinz was playin' WWF! Ain't nothin' in that room for an eight-year-old. That is a good room for good company. No, Jeffy don't count as company. Why don't you go down Jeffy's house and jump on his parents' furniture for a while?

WATCHING *WRESTLEMANIA*

I ordered the kids the new *WrestleMania* the other day. Damn near seventy dollars! For that price I could get Hacksaw Jim Duggan to fight the Honky Tonk Man in my cellar, then have them clean out the gutters. It started out OK with Hulk Hogan, the Rock, and Stone Cold all in the ring. Then all they do is talk and drink beer. I says, "Is this *WrestleMania* or *Cheers*?" I half expected Frasier to come running down and slide into the ring. Hulk Hogan didn't even tear his shirt off! What, is he cutting back on shirt expenses? For seventy dollars you better be ripping off shirts, tearing the apron apart, eating turnbuckles.

I liked it better when wrestlers had great character names, like Bret "The Hitman" Hart, the Million Dollar Man, and Sgt. Slaughter. Now they just use their real names, like Brad, Cody, and Justin. Is this *WrestleMania* or a boy band?

They had one of them thirty-man royal-battle matches! People was just running around knocking people over, punching each other. It's like Walmart on Black Friday.

And Kane, his wrestling costume ain't nothing but dress slacks. He looked like he come straight from his niece's christening and hopped in the ring.

AT KARATE CLASS

No, Brandon, you ain't quitting after one class. Just 'cause they ain't letting you whip around Chinese stars and throw Hadokens. No wonder the sensei wanted a month's pay up front. You were in there for an hour.

COACHING LITTLE LEAGUE

Before the game starts, let's get a couple things straight: No, you can't run home to go to the bathroom. No, we can't take a time-out so you can run to the snack shack. No, we can't just play soccer instead. And no, Joey, you can't switch teams in the middle of a game.

Look at the pitcher for the other team. What is he, eighteen? He's got a mustache! Looks like Tom Selleck playing out there. I swear half of that team drove themselves to the game today.

Slide, Michael! Whaddya mean you don't wanna get your uniform dirty? You going to Red Lobster after this?

Guys, it's a fly ball, not a live grenade!

Jeffy, where'd you find a snow cone in left field?

Whaddya mean you think you're done playing? You're tired? That's 'cause you went swimming today, didn't you?

Hey, Mandy, what are you doing behind that dugout?! We're here to see your brother get to first base, not your boyfriend.

Are you kids losing just so we can get to Dairy Queen faster?

You don't gotta cry 'cause you struck out. If anyone should be crying, it's me. We got twelve more games left.

LITTLE LEAGUE TEAM
AT DAIRY QUEEN

Your choices are small chocolate or vanilla cones. Don't be up there ordering Full Meal Deals. No, you can't order a whole cup of jimmies.

Hey, Joey, that small cone sure looks like chicken fingers to me.

Now, what'd I tell yinz all to bring to the game? Your parents' Entertainment Book coupons; pass 'em up.

I don't care if Hunter's dad takes their team to Cold Stone. He works down Google; he can afford to throw money away.

Paul, it takes you ten minutes to run in from left field, but someone says "Blizzard," and you're up here faster than that "Insane Bolt."

What, Paul? Do they have lettuce wraps?! Yeah, over at Dairy Queen's famous soup and salad bar. Would you like to see a wine list as well?

Does the ice cream have soy in it?! No, it's got jimmies; get going.

There's no reason that six of yinz should be going in the bathroom at the same time.

Jeffy, how'd you get your inhaler to pump out butterscotch? Since they don't put Dennis the Menace on the cups no more, they ought to use Jeffy the Jaggo.

This is the only team I know that gets more ice cream on their uniforms than dirt.

TRADING STUFF

Brandon, where's your hat? You traded it? For what? A Dairy Queen Dilly Bar?! What'd I tell you about trading things? First, you traded your bike for some Lemonheads. Then your book bag for a Wacky Wall Walker. And your Nintendo for the ride on the back of a dirt bike. I had to nullify all that.

Sources are telling me that you traded your Xbox for a Chinese star, Silly Bandz, and a Skylander to be named later.

WATCHING THE PITTSBURGH PIRATES

JULY: Pirates are gonna win the World Series!

AUGUST: They're at least gonna make the playoffs. Wild-card spot.

SEPTEMBER: Please just finish over .500! That too much to ask?! Brandon, go get the old Nintendo. I gotta see the Pirates win *something*.

All right, guys, get around the Clemente statue. No, that ain't Barry Bonds, it's Roberto Clemente! If it was Barry Bonds, it'd just be a statue of a giant bottle of pills.

Who the hell cares 'bout them stupid stats? "He's batting .382 in the month of September after a rain delay during home games after his wife has just had a baby."

Of course Mandy needs a ride home from the mall during the game. They sell beds at the mall, right? Problem solved.

I need to take money out of the 401(k) for the Bucco tickets. The stress these teams put me through, I'll never live to see retirement anyhows.

BASEBALL TICKETS

Jeffy, put that "I Need Tickets" sign down. Keep it up and you'll need a sign that says you need a ride home.

RUNNING A MARATHON

You need inspiration to finish running the marathon? Just imagine Freddy Krueger is chasing you. Or Ray Lewis.

Only way you could get your mum to run a marathon is if there were free Yankee Candles at the end of it.

You need fifty dollars to do the Color Run? You can run around in the backyard and I'll throw some flour and food coloring at ya. It's the same thing.

THE NEIGHBOR'S YARD

Hey, Tom, you ever think about cutting that grass of yours? Your yard is making my house look bad. It looks like the world from *Avatar* over there. I ain't never seen a driveway that has to be mowed. All the kids think a witch lives in your house. Ain't you ever wondered why the band never comes to sell you hoagies?

Just look at all them dandelions. You got all them fuzzies floating over here, giving my kids allergies. We're going through Claritin like they was Necco Wafers.

I seen a UPS guy try to deliver a package to your house.

Had to turn around. Didn't have a machete. And they still ain't found that paperboy.

You might as well carve out a labyrinth and charge admission! Then again, who the hell would want to get to the end of that maze! "What's at the end of the maze? A jag-off."

And pick up all them crab apples! They been lying there all mushy so long they're starting to ferment. Smells like liquor over there.

If a coma patient woke up and the first thing he saw was your house, he wouldn't know what time of year it was, 'cause you still got every damn holiday decoration up. Had that manger scene in your yard since Christmas. It looks like baby Jesus was born in *Jurassic Park*.

And what an eyesore that big shiny yard globe is. What do you mean it's good luck? Does it know you drive a '91 Tempo?

Yeah, I read somewhere that screens work best when they are laying *underneath* a window.

JEHOVAH'S WITNESSES

Brandon, get in the house! Turn the TV off. Everybody get down. Don't move, don't even breathe. I seen Jehovah's Witnesses comin' up the street. No, there ain't no fire, it's Jehovah's Witnesses. Why would I have told you to run *into* the house if there was a fire? Next time listen when Smokey the Bear is talking at school.

Deb, turn the fish tank off. I'm not taking no chances. If they know we're in here, they'll stay out there waiting all night. They're like Tremors. We might as well use the same drill we got for tornados and get down the cellar.

Yes, it is too them, Deb! Out there wearing white shirts, black ties, and briefcases. Who you think that is, Don Draper?

Why can't they be like our church and don't talk to anyone? That ain't what religion is about, talking. It's about sitting and standing. We got our beliefs already. What's next? Ray Lewis gonna stop over looking to convert us into Ravens fans?

I don't care if they wanna share "the Good News." The only good news I wanna hear is that Rax is coming back. Uncle Alligator knocks on the door and it's a different story.

They're always talking about Armageddon, and not even the good one with Bruce Willis. We already had our Armageddon. It was called last winter.

Deb, your solution to everything is to "just be nice." When the hell has that ever worked out for anyone?

They don't buy no Christmas, birthday, or Easter gifts. Then again, maybe we should hear what they have to say.

THE "FURRIES"

No, Deb, you were wrong, that weren't no mascot convention. Them were furries! Bunch of idiots dressed up as animals. The kids was hoping to get a picture with Mickey or

Goofy. All they had there was a bunch of wolves hugging each other. I shoulda known something was up as soon as I seen the cars was being valet parked by a hippopotamus dressed as a cowboy.

I seen a German shepherd nuzzlin' with a unicorn. There was a horse in a bra and underwear. A gazelle in jean shorts. A husky dog in a Buffalo Sabres jersey. I was half expecting to see Chuck E. Cheese makin' out with Tony the Tiger.

See, this is what happens when them kids look on the Internet.

There was a Bengals furry and a Ravens furry. I was praying for a Polamalu furry to come and take 'em out!

One guy tells me he spent three grand on his furry costume! I said you coulda spent $29.99 down that Halloween store that takes over the empty Sears every year.

That guy that works down at that hoagie place? Seen him dressed like a fox, sitting in a corner, licking himself. I says to the kids, "Don't touch nothin'. You'll get rabies."

The kids run up to a giant penguin, thought it was for the hockey team. Until it started rolling around on the ground with a gorilla in a business suit.

I'll never look at that Pirate Parrot the same way. At least he shoots T-shirts at ya!

If this is what mascots do, I'd hate to see them Pierogies down at PNC Park after hours. Onions and cheese all over the place. Clint Hurdle comes in, don't know what the hell happened.

And then they had a dance competition there. You ever seen a goat break dancing?

I seen one guy dressed as a dog lift his leg to pee. I had to hit him with a newspaper! You don't pee in a convention center. There's a baseball-card show here next weekend.

I was hoping Bob Barker would show up, get 'em all spayed and neutered.

Then this kitty cat pack surrounds me and the kids, meowing at us. I needed a spray bottle to get outta there! One guy, dressed as a dog, kept talking to me about landscaping. Wouldn't shut up. I had to fake-throw a ball to get him out of there.

I tell you, you don't see any of this down the auto show. Cars rubbing up and down against each other. No, guys don't rub up and down on their cars, Deb. They're buffing and waxing them.

AT THE ZOO

We don't need nothing from the snack bar. I swear, the only animals yinz are interested in seeing are Goldfish crackers, Teddy Grahams, and Zebra Cakes.

What's this? A snow leopard?! After last winter I don't want to see anything with snow. How's 'bout we find a beach leopard? Or a partly cloudy leopard.

Look, Brandon, there's a raccoon. Now we don't gotta pay to see that *Guardians of the Galaxy*.

Look at the flamingers. They're like the plastic ones in Tom's yard. Except they ain't covered in mold. No, Jeffy, don't feed the flamingers Alka-Seltzer. That's all I need is them blowing up, and the zoo putting them on my tab.

These lions sleep twenty-one hours a day. Almost as much as your sister.

Vegas odds are saying these zoo lions will win a Super Bowl before the Detroit Lions.

Whaddya mean the turtles are boring? Just 'cause they ain't whipping around numchucks and eating pizza, you kids don't care about 'em.

No, kids, that ain't Aunt Linda's bathing suit, that's a leopard.

Rick, ain't no one care that you can kill a deer faster than a leopard. Give the leopard a semiautomatic weapon and expired hunting tags and he'll give you a run for your money. How's come you base every living thing's value on how fast it can kill deer?

Are they CGI?! Those are real elephants, Brandon. How's about we lay off the video games a few days.

No, we ain't putting quarters in the viewfinder. Look, I found the view . . . for free.

Brandon, no staring contests with the silverback gorilla! That's how *Planet of the Apes* happened.

We can't skip the penguins. Morgan Freeman wouldn't like it. It says here that penguins eat fish, spend half their life in the ocean, and lose after only one round in the playoffs.

What animal would I like to be? An electric eel. It's the only animal that don't get a power bill. I'm surprised the power company don't got a meter attached to that eel, charging him for making his own electricity.

The male seahorse has the babies. No, that can't happen in humans. Unless you're that Kyle and Brian couple that live next door to your gram.

No, don't taunt the polar bears. Yeah, Jeffy, go in there and offer him a Coke and see what happens. What the hell is Al Gore talking about? These polar bears look fine.

Don't pet the deer. 'Cause you know what's next right? Ticks! How do I know?! Well, 'cause that one's eating week-old Arby's and the other one's running around with a used Band-Aid in its mouth. Don't even let Uncle Rick walk by the deer exhibit. He'll end up setting up a tree stand.

What, Jessica? Do they have a Hippogriff?! Yeah, sure, they keep him over with the minotaurs and the unicorn.

No, we ain't getting nothing from the gift shop. You got all these *real* animals to look at and you kids are more fascinated with stuffed animals. If I took yinz to Niagara Falls you'd be off playing in a puddle.

THE CAT

How's come when the cat is doing something destructive in my house, yinz guys' first instinct ain't to stop it, but to start filming?

Got a whole kitchen of linoleum, but every time that cat throws up, he finds the little rug by the sink.

Keep that cat outta my chair. There's about enough hair on it to build a whole 'nother cat!

THE DOG

You kids should be thankful I even let yinz keep a dog. My dad used to say, "This ain't really working out" and take pets back to the store.

How's come the dog deliberately waits till the Pens are on a power play before it wants me to let it outside?

MOTHER'S DAY

You kids need to buy something *really* special for your mum this year. Like a Pepperidge Farm cake.

FATHER'S DAY

Do kids get presents on Father's Day?! Yeah, I got yinz five bags of mulch. Get going.

AT THE MALL

All right, yinz can walk around by yourselves. But don't leave the mall, talk to strangers, or go in the sexy section in Spencer's.

Deb, I'm putting a two-candle limit on them Yankee

Candles. You're gonna have the whole house smelling like Apple Breeze and November Rain.

TAKING PROM PICTURES

Sure, Mandy, you can go to prom with an eighteen-year-old. I just need his name, address, and five minutes alone with him in the Octagon.

Mandy, come on out here so's we can get some nice pictures of you in your dress. Or do you have to throw the bathroom breaker another eight times before you're done with that hair dryer? Them dials down at the power company are just spinning.

Andrew, how did you find a tuxedo with a hoodie on it?! I guess I should at least be happy you're not going as Tim Burton's *Corpse Bride* again. What did *I* wear to prom? A Terry Bradshaw jersey.

Linda, how many times you gonna fiddle with her hair? You got a hundred bobby pins in there; it ain't gonna move. You want me to go down and get the caulking gun? I said *caulking* gun, Jeffy, so quit laughing.

No, Deb we ain't taking pictures with your cell phone 'cause I never see 'em. You end up getting a new phone and them pictures is gone forever. Like the one you lost

of me and that guy that looked just like Roy Scheider. When the hell am I ever gonna see him again?! Once in a lifetime opportunity, gone.

Jessica, quit pouting. You'll go to the prom one day. You act like Mandy's going to some magic fairy castle with Prince Charming. She's eating dinner down the Sheraton, for crying out loud.

Don't ruin that dress either, Mandy, 'cause that's your dowry. That dress cost you one year of college. We was gonna send you to Penn State. You've been downgraded to University of Phoenix. That dress better keep you cool this summer 'cause now we ain't running no air-conditioning. Instead of vacation this summer, we're all gonna sit around and stare at the dress for a week.

Geez, how many kids you got stuffed into that limo?! Looks like one of them Chinese subways. And what's that smoke coming out the moon roof? Your prom will be over before it even starts!

Who's that kid with the beard? How old is he? Is that Dan Wilkins? He went to *my* prom!

Who's this little girl getting out of the limo? Can't be more than three years old. What do you mean it's Michelle and Mike's baby? That better be the only baby coming outta that prom!

CAMPING IN THE BACKYARD

OK, you got your lantern, sleeping bags, portable Nintendos, cooler of pop, and just about every pillow and blanket from the house. You're really roughing it, Davy Crockett. You think maybe you'll make it past nine thirty this time?

No, you ain't bringing out the good couch cushions to sleep on. And what are yinz putting that coffee table in there for? That tent is starting to look like an IKEA! What else yinz got in there? The papasan chair?! Put that back or Mum is gonna kill ya. I might as well put the fridge out there and have Comcast come out and connect cable. You want a wireless router, too? You're the only kids I know that have to watch Netflix while camping.

If you are going to camp then *camp*. Stop looking through the window at me and Mum watching TV. And I want that tent put away bright and early tomorrow or it's gonna kill my grass. It's still brown over there from last year. Last time yinz left the tent out, that bad thunderstorm blew it away to the Land of Oz. And don't just throw it behind the shed. Or you know what's next, right? Potato bugs.

Quit comin' in and out of the house to pee. Go behind the shed. Oh, you gotta go number two? Do that in Tom's yard.

Jeffy, if you're gonna spray OFF! on your face, at least close your eyes. You sprayed so much, you're flammable. Don't get too close to that citronella candle.

No, yinz can't walk down to 7-Eleven to get a can of Jolt. Get back in the tent. I'd send yinz out on a snipe hunt but with my luck, Jeffy, you'd find it.

Keep that tent clean. 'Cause if your mum keeps buying all them Vera Bradley purses, we're gonna be living in it.

THE SCREEN DOOR

In or out! If I have to hear this screen door slam one more time, I'm bolting it shut.

And quit pushing on the screen to open the door. You're gonna put your hand right through it.

THE ICE-CREAM MAN

You don't hear me yelling for dinner, but them ice-cream bells could wake yinz out of a coma. Did you remember to open the screen door this time? Or did you just burst through it again like a varsity football team?

We got a whole freezer of Bomb Pops and yinz won't touch 'em 'cause they stick to the wrapper. You just got to blow in them. Or is that too much work?

Let me guess where yinz got the money: the First National Bank of Dad's Change Jar? My change jar is putting the ice-cream man's kids through college. I had a Sacagawea dollar and a framed set of state quarters. Them's all gone. Right down to the Goody Bar man.

Why does that ice-cream man look like he lives *in* the ice-cream truck? The amount of ice cream you kids buy, he don't even drive around anymore, he just comes right to our house. Look outside in the middle of the night, see him sitting in the driveway like *Cape Fear*.

THE SLIP 'N SLIDE

Hey, who the hell told yinz you could put the Slip 'n Slide in my backyard? You're gonna kill the grass! You remember what happened last year when yinz put the tent out for a week? There's still a big brown spot over there.

Is that Mum's good dishwashing soap, too? Making the

Slip 'n Slide all slippy and sudsy? Oh, I'd hate to be you. I'd hate to be you when she comes home and sees that.

CATCHING LIGHTNING BUGS

Hey, quit whackin' the lightning bugs with a Wiffle Ball bat. That's cruel. You're supposed to bottle them in the little jar. I don't care if Jeffy's dad says he's allowed. He's an idiot. Buys DVDs down Barnes & Noble's.

And where did yinz get them jars? If I go in the house and find a sink full of pickles, jelly, and Miracle Whip, we got problems.

Deb, whaddya mean it's animal cruelty to catch 'em? That's what lightning bugs are for. They're born, they light up a few times, then *poof*, their butts become kids' rings. Animal cruelty. We had ribs for dinner. You think the cow was just letting us borrow them?

THE FREEZER

No, we ain't putting lightning bugs in the freezer. I swear, when you kids don't know what to do with something, your first thought is "put it in the freezer." Glow sticks from last Halloween. Color-changer action figures. Snowballs from last winter. I half expect to go in there and find the Demolition Man. It's a freezer, not a cryogenic chamber. Same thing happened to Walt Disney. He died, his kids didn't know what the hell to do with him, threw him in a freezer.

Hey, Deb, these flashlight batteries are still good. Stick 'em in the freezer.

SWIMMING POOLS

How's come all year I gotta flicker the lights to wake yinz up, but in summer you're already playing Marco Polo by seven a.m.?

Did yinz warsh your feet off in that little bucket beside the pool before you got in the pool? I don't want grass clippings clogging up that filter. I swear this pool got more beetles than Volkswagen.

No, I ain't buying yinz any more alligator rafts. They got a life expectancy of three and a half minutes.

I know it's cold; just stay in the water and you'll get used to it. Or play *Titanic*.

No, Great-Grandma can't go swimming. This ain't the *Cocoon* pool.

Brandon, keep the indoor toys out of the pool. I got the entire Jedi Council clogging up my filter.

No, you ain't going into the house to pee. Just go behind the shed.

Jeffy, you ain't gonna get dysentery. It's a chlorinated pool, not the Oregon Trail. Believe me, the only disease in the water is you.

No, you kids ain't going "night swimming." That's reserved for me, Mum, and Sade on the boombox.

THE GARAGE

Hey, Brandon, quit smacking around the tennis ball hanging in the garage. That ain't a toy, Andre Agassi. That's to stop Mum from bumping the car into the lawn mower.

DAD'S TOOLS

Hey, where are all my tools? Well, I'm missing stuff. What are yinz doing out in the street with them? Building a bike ramp?! Oh, no you're not. I'll ramp yinz right to your room. You ride your bike off that thing and you'll be going up a lot more ramps . . . in a wheelchair. You're trying to break a record?! What record? The quickest to send Dad to the nuthouse?

Do I have to refresh your memory from last year when yinz built that shoddy tree house in the backyard that collapsed

after an hour? Now you're out here trying to build something that's going to launch you through the air. That Pinewood Derby car yinz built last year burst into flames right out of the gate. I don't know how yinz did it, but you done it. Weren't even any gasoline in the damn thing. The troop leader said he ain't seen nothing like that in his twenty years in the Boy Scouts.

Jeffy, that level ain't a Lightsaber! You're going to break that bubble and I'm going to break your head. Yinz must be on a record pace to ruin everything I own. I don't know why I even bother to buy anything new.

Where'd you get this "ramp" idea at anyways? *Jackass*?

Why would yinz need to watch *Jackass* when you live right next door to Tom? Every time you and Jeffy watch that YouTube, we end up having to go to MedExpress. You'll end up breaking your arm and having to wear a cast. Then you can't go swimming all summer. That means no jackknives, no cannonballs, no belly flops. Think this through, boys.

Why don't yinz ever do this dangerous stuff down Jeffy's house? That's all I need is the news coming here asking me why every kid in the neighborhood leaves my house with broken limbs. I need to start buying "Jeffy insurance."

And also, where did yinz get all that wood for the ramp? A building site?! You can't just take wood from a building site! You're gonna go to jail for that. I'll stop all this right now, I'll tell your mum. I would not want to be you when she comes out here and sees that ramp. Jeffy's mom don't even care what he does. She's down their house just sipping White Zinfandel all day.

GOING DOWN THE CRICK

Hey, what are yinz doin' playing in the crick? Didn't you hear me calling your name for supper? Your sister made it home, why couldn't you?

I don't care if yinz are building another shack. No, you ain't eating your dinner in it. And who was cussing? I could hear it from the street. That's all you hear coming out of these woods is cussing and dirt bikes. I don't want you talking to them kids on the dirt bikes. Don't take any rides or anything else they offer you.

And stay away from that fire pit and dirty couches the teenagers got set up. Ain't enough shots at MedExpress to cure ya from the diseases those will give ya. Them teenagers are always partying down here. Who the hell would ever want to go to a party at a crick? Where do they celebrate Christmas, in the sewer?

Why is your Xbox down here?! Look at all this stuff yinz brought down! You got the Speak & Spell, the *Ghostbusters* Firehouse, and Crocodile Mile all set up. Hills Department Store ain't where the toys are, the *crick* is where the toys are.

And Pat Coll, what are you doing down here? Ain't there no cricks in Munhall? Well, did you at least tell your mum this time so's we don't hear another Amber Alert like when you wandered off last spring? Found you playing in one of them fake kids' rooms in IKEA. It's easier to find Waldo than Pat Coll. Your mum needs to tie a little cat bell around your neck.

Better not let Mum catch you using her good butter knives to get the mud out of your tennis shoes.

Your clothes stink! Take them off down here and come back home in your underwear. Ain't no one going to see ya.

And when you get home knock on the door and I'll just spray you down with the hose.

PLAYING IN THE WOODS

Hey, be careful back there. There's jagger bushes all over. You're gonna get bristles and burrs all over your socks and shoelaces. You know what, there's sinkholes all through them woods so you better just come on in. That's all I need is you falling in an old mine. No, you ain't gonna "find gold and gems." It's dirty old coal mines, not One-Eyed Willie's pirate ship.

Let's go, we're having dinner. What do you mean you've been eating honeysuckles and berries?! You wouldn't eat a grape after it fell on the kitchen floor, but you'll chow down on some plants you found down by the crick?

Look at them clothes! Did yinz even try to leave any dirt in the woods?

PLAYING AT THE END
OF THE DAY

Hey, guys, it's getting dark, so watch out for Mum's clothesline! You run into that, it'll take your head right off. Like them speeder-bike guys in *Return of the Jedi*. Ewoks didn't set it up, Mum did.

Hey, Deb, let's get these kids outta here. I give it five minutes before the sleepover requests start coming.

Jessica, I told you ten minutes ago when you asked if Dana could sleep over that *we'll see*. Well, I ain't done seeing yet, so quit bugging me. Ask me one more time and I'm canceling lightning bugs.

All right, Brandon, get up in the tub. No, swimming today don't count. You're covered in glowing lightning-bug guts like you was fighting the Predator.

AT THE DRIVE-IN

See, at the drive-in ya get two movies for seven bucks. Here we got *Iron Man*. Turn around, there's *The Great Gratsby*. *What's Fast Is Furious*. *Hungover 3*. What do you mean they don't let you switch screens? They ain't gonna know 'cause I'll be in stealth mode . . . headlights off.

Linda, you don't remember the first movie you saw at the drive-in? I'll bet I know the second: *She's Having a Baby*.

No, Brandon, stay away from that fogged-up car. That car's rated R. That smell? Uh, them kids are just burning leaves . . . in their car . . . with the windows up.

No, you don't need no glow-in-the-dark bracelets. Just go catch a lightning bug and rub it on your wrist.

Linda and Rick brought a couch?! All they need is a coffee table and they'll have a whole Showcase Showdown.

No, you kids ain't walking over to KMart's. What for? Pool noodles?! What could you possibly need pool noodles for right now?

Mandy, who are them guys and why do none of them have sleeves? No, no, no, tell *The Outsiders* to hit the road. But first ask 'em if they have a cigarette for Uncle Rick.

Brandon, just go pee in the woods. No, we ain't looking at you, we're watching Robert Downey fight this guy made out of fire.

Yinz are getting too close to the cars. Play ball over by the swings. Say hi to Danny Zucco. Keep talking back to me and you'll be "stranded at the drive-in."

THE DRIVE-IN SNACK BAR

You don't need a cup just 'cause Superman's on it. He don't make the pop taste better. And no Angry Birds candy. Keep asking, and all you're getting is Angry Dad.

Quit grabbing at stuff. I swear your eyes is lighting up like you're immigrants seeing Ellis Island for the first time.

No, you ain't getting no Garbage Pail Kids. Last time yinz

brought 'em to school and caused a huge stir. Mum and I had to sign all them forms just so you could go back. The church had a prayer circle for yinz that Sunday.

No, Linda, they ain't gonna take a check. Where you think you are, Montgomery Ward's?

How's come anytime you kids see a railing your first instinct is to start swinging on it?

Hey, Jeffy, any reason why you're putting hot butter on your Sour Patch Kids?

THE AVENGERS

You got Captain America, the Hulk, Thor, Iron Man, some woman, and Robin Hood. What the hell is Robin Hood gonna do? If we need an apple shot off of somebody's head, we'll give you a call.

And you should see the size of Lou Ferrigno in *The Avengers*. He's gotta be taking supplements or something.

Geez, that Samuel L. Jackson is in everything these days. I half expected him to show up in my daughter's communion video.

The kids are gonna build their own Iron Man suit? These

are the same kids that took two weeks to figure out how to set up that Mouse Trap game.

After the movie I bought Brandon one of them Captain America shields. Not five minutes after we get home, it's on the roof. Along with the web shooters, a Lightsaber, and a Batarang. I got the whole *Avengers* arsenal up there.

I'll tell you my ultimate *Avengers* team: Robocop, Indiana Jones, Hulk Hogan, Rocky Balboa, and for the woman . . . the evil robot lady from *Superman III*.

BATMAN MOVIES

I took the kids to see that new Batman Part Three last night. *The Dark Knight Rises*. How was it? I'm not sure 'cause it's probably still going on right now. Wherever the Dark Knight is rising to, it took him three hours to do it. Only thing rising in that movie is ticket prices.

Right at the beginning of the movie, Bruce Wayne quits being Batman. I says, "What the hell's this movie about, then?" If that Kristen Bale don't want to be Batman, put Michael Keaton in there. Batman was in that movie for a whole ten minutes. I seen more Batman in an episode of *Scooby-Doo!*

Uncle Rick hates Batman's new outfit? Strong words from the guy whose entire wardrobe was bought with Marlboro Miles.

I tell ya what, if I was the president, my first order of business would be to shut that Gotham City the hell down! Scarecrows, clowns, evil wrestlers . . . way too much trouble coming from outta there. "Mr. President, we got another problem." "Let me guess: Gotham City. I'm nuking it."

SUPERMAN: MAN OF STEEL

I took the kids down to see that new Superman Part Six. They call it *Man of Steel*. At first I was excited because I thought we were seeing a movie about Mean Joe Greene.

Them moviemakers were too cheap to even give Superman his red underwear.

Superman and this General Zod kept throwing each other through building after building. After a while, I thought, Maybe the buildings are the bad guys? And this Superman with no underwear, he don't save nobody. He levels the whole city of Metropolis and kills thousands of people. So, basically, he did the supervillains' job for them! "Well, Superman killed everyone. Now what the hell are we supposed to do?" The next *Avengers* movie should be them coming to stop Superman! If you ever fall off a building and you see this Superman without his underwear coming, you tell him to just keep on flying. You got a better chance with the pavement.

Margot Kidder's Lois Lane was way better. She drank,

screamed, and punched. And that was before the director even said "Action!"

Hey, Brandon, don't be playing Superman with mum's good towels! Them is for holidays. I can see the little holly and berries on them from here! Use them greasy paint towels down in the garage.

AT THE FOURTH OF JULY PARADE

What do you mean I can't leave a chair to save my spot two weeks before the parade? That's what chairs are for! Christopher Columbus, first thing he done when he got outta the boat is put a chair down for the new country.

I can't drink beer at the parade 'cause the police are coming down the sidewalk? Who do you think I got the beer from?!

When I was a kid, they used to have a bear ride a little motorcycle off a little ramp. He'd come over and give you a cigar. Tell you the score of the Pirate game. He came over the house, kissed Grandma on the side of the mouth. Then he bit someone and they put him down.

If yinz gotta go to the bathroom, run over to the church over there. I know you're Catholic, but you're still allowed. What is it, Lutheran? Same thing.

Hey, Ron, how the hell did you get in the parade? Just 'cause you have a PT Cruiser with a flag on it?

What do you mean, the parade is only half over? It's been two hours! This Fourth of July parade is gonna end up the Labor Day parade.

No, we're not stopping at any of them little road stands to get fireworks. We get the good fireworks. From that guy's trunk in Ohio.

THE FOURTH OF JULY

Hey, you better not be lighting them black snakes on my driveway! You're gonna stain it. Grab a block of wood from behind the shed.

We ain't lighting fireworks yet, it's still light out. When you see lightning bugs, then it's time. Go throw them bang-snaps. Or light them little tanks. Ask me one more time 'bout them fireworks and I'm canceling the Fourth of July. All you'll get to see in the sky is heat lightning.

Hey, you blowin' up them G.I. Joes with them firecrackers? Well, I ain't buyin' yinz new ones, so you better figure out how to get them legs back on.

I got a game for yinz. It's called Clean Up All the Pop Cans. Winner gets to eat.

Jessica, go pour Pap another beer from the keg. Yes, you can play bartender, but no playing *Ghostbusters* and spraying people like last year.

Hey, Rick, I don't care if you made them yourself, how's about laying off the M80s for a while? You're gonna make Pap think he's back in Vietnam. You'll give him that P . . . STD syndrome. He'll end up tackling Brandon's little Asian friend.

No, Mum, nobody got shot, it was an M80. No, it ain't Bingo. There ain't even an *m* in Bingo.

Why are you kids jumping off the wall with the patio umbrella? Trying to float?! I'll float ya right up to time-out, Mary Poppins! How's that sound?

Can we go five minutes without a kid crying?

Hey, Tom, who the hell plays Sarah McLachlan on the Fourth of July? Geez, my animals are crying over here. Is that whole iPod set to "jag-off"?

No, Deb, I ain't going over to Tom's to "borrow" ice. How the hell are we gonna "borrow" it? Give him back the water?

You don't want Tom's ice anyhows. The drinks will taste like loser.

We're out of freeze pops? That's 'cause you didn't let them freeze, you just drank 'em. Time to get out the Snoopy Sno Cone Machine and start cranking.

LIGHTING SPARKLERS

Light your sparklers off of each other's. Or just use Gram's cigarette.

Can't yinz just hold the sparklers? You don't need to do cartwheels with them or have Lightsaber battles. Now, go out in the yard and find all the stuff that landed. That's all I need is to step on a hot sparkler. Mum put out a coffee tin of water; you dip it in. Where did Jeffy run off to with his sparkler? Guess we'll just listen for the sirens.

Go downtown to see fireworks?! Nah, you can see 'em just fine from the grocery-store parking lot.

PLAYING OUTSIDE

Why are yinz wearing them big winter coats in the middle of July? That looks suspicious. You're shooting each other with BB Guns?! I swear it'll be a miracle if you live to see middle school.

DRIVING TO VACATION

Mandy, you don't need makeup to ride in a car. You expecting paparazzi at the gas station?

Hey Deb, you put them stick-figure family decals on my car and you can take the mum one right back off, 'cause you'll be out the door.

You gotta pee already?! We ain't even off our own street! I told yinz no bathroom stops till you can smell the ocean.

No, we don't got a DVD player, we got windows. Sit and look.

About to pass a Volkswagen dealership with tons of Beetles in the lot. These punch-buggy kids are going to be boxing each other!

The hotel room only got two beds, so you girls are sharing and Brandon will sleep on a chair. He'll be fine. I seen him sleep under the coffee table.

Why did I lock all the doors?! Why the hell would you be trying to open them when the car is moving is the bigger question!

The seat-belt strap goes over your shoulder, not under your arm. I don't care if it itches your neck; just stop being a pain in mine!

Look at these two rigs taking up both lanes. Yeah, you kids can give them the sign to honk their horns. I'm going to give them another sign.

Deb, what does your sister know about directions? I'll let her know if I need to find the nearest T.J.Maxx. Only person I know that could find a T.J.Maxx at the Grand Canyon.

FIGHTING IN THE CAR

Quit fighting back there. I don't care who started it, I'm ending it. Tell you what: just pretend there's an invisible line between yinz, and don't cross it. I spy with my little eye a boy that's gonna get smacked in the mouth if he don't stop tormenting his sister. If I hear any more crying or screaming, I'm turning the car around. Vacation canceled. I'll go fishing. There'll be three red butts sitting on the side of the road. See that big building up there? That's the orphanage. I'll drop all you kids off.

What do you mean I'm angry?! I'm angry 'cause you kids did it to me. Before you come along, I was the most laid-back guy I knew.

MAKING GOOD TIME

We ain't stopping at McDonald's, Burger King, Dairy Queen, Toys "R" Us, or Children's Palace. I'm trying to make good time. Only stop we're making is the beer distributor, 'cause it's way cheaper than buying it down the shore.

Deb, you told me to go this way and now I gotta get on a toll road. Looks like we just lost one night of eating out.

No more air-conditioning. It's usin' up all my gas.

ON A BEACH VACATION

Now, before you kids do or touch anything, ask yourself a question: "Will this cost Dad money?" I don't have any more change for the pop machine. If you're thirsty, yinz can go swimming and open your mouth. No, we ain't paying $5.99 to watch *Wreck-It-Ralph* at the hotel. Uncle Rick had ten beers and he's bumping into lounge chairs. Go watch *Wreck-It-Rick* for free.

And make sure yinz don't leave nothing laying out. It'll be stolen. There's gypsies all over here. Stay away from anyone with long earrings and tambourines, running in a circle. First they're braiding your hair, then you're in the back of a van, missing organs. I don't want this family's first TV appearance to be *Unsolved Mysteries*.

PROPER BEACH ATTIRE

Linda, quit walking around here like you're Bo Derek in *10*. You look more like Morgan Freeman in *Seven*.

Pap, don't you think it's about time to get rid of that one-piece bathing suit? You look like a high-school wrestler.

No, we ain't going down the store so you can get them naughty T-shirts. Like the WHO FARTED? T-shirt? We all know it was Pap.

SWIMMING IN THE OCEAN

Jessica, don't scream like that just 'cause a piece of seaweed touched your foot. You save that scream for when you see sharks, jellyfish, or Ray Lewis.

SOUVENIRS

No hermit crabs this year. That one you bought last year got too big for its shell and didn't know what the hell to do. It had to move into one of your bronze baby shoes. Now the TV room smells like Red Lobster.

We're not buying seashells. You got a whole beach of them. Next, you'll be wanting to buy sand.

And don't hose your grandma out of money when I said no. She gets one check a month. And you already had her buy you that grain of rice with your name on it.

CELEBRITY SIGHTING

Hey, Deb, guess who I found out is in our hotel. "Small Wonder!" Yeah, she works at the pool bar now. I'm gonna go get her autograph. And a piña colada.

AT THE CHURCH BAZAAR

I don't know about these rides. This one has got kids on it and the guy ain't even finished putting it together yet. No, Brandon, don't try climbing out of the Ferris wheel. The ride operator just went for a smoke; he'll be back. That thing been spinning for a half hour. Gives a whole new definition to "ride all day pass."

Hey, Sister Evelyn, you might want to say an extra rosary before you get on that UFO ride!

No, you kids ain't going in that dunk tank. 'Cause the only prize it's giving out is pink eye.

Jessica, here's a couple tickets, go get me a beer. What am I gonna *pay* you?! You can have a sip on the way back. But don't let Father or the nuns see ya. Or worse yet, your mum.

No, that ain't a Zoltar machine. That's just Clint Schumacher passed out in the blackjack booth with his mouth open. Go ahead, flip a quarter in his mouth and see if you get your wish.

I ain't giving yinz no more quarters. I'm saving them for the Chuck-a-luck wheel. Go ask Gram. Where the hell do you think she is? Been playing Bingo since nine a.m. Just blowing through that Social Security check. If I were you, I wouldn't count on any Christmas presents from her this year.

Here's a few dollars for you to play a game called Go Get Pap Some Haluski.

Hey, Deb, how's about you don't spend our entire tax return in the White Elephant sale this year?

Someone better keep an eye on Father Tim at that poker table, or else next Sunday he'll need to pass around a third and fourth collection basket. Hey, Father, with all this money the church is takin' in, thinking about maybe buyin' some cushions for them pews?

If they's giving out goldfish, then you might wanna win

ten. Maybe one of them will actually make it home alive this year.

OK, yinz guys can go in the church to pee. But that ain't a free pass to go running around in there, putting on the altar-boy robes to play ghosts.

Jeffy just bought a round of darts for the balloon game. Hey, Sister Ruth, you're about to earn that dollar.

No, Mandy, I ain't giving you sixteen dollars so's you and Andrew can get your caricature drawn. Give it a few days and the police will be sketching Andrew for free.

Deb, there's no way in hell we're using that ATM they got set up. That thing will charge your card a service fee just for walking past it.

Old Phyllis Fletcher brought that box of kittens here to try to unload them on some sucker. No, Deb, put them hissing devils back!

USING AIR-CONDITIONING

You got the air-conditioning running all night long and you're sleeping under blankets? You might as well keep warm by just burning money.

SUMMER READING

No, Brandon, reading the *Rats of Nimh* Wikipedia page don't count as your summer reading.

GOING TO SCHOOL

You lost your backpack already?! Well, grab one of them free grocery-store "book bags" from under the sink and don't forget to double-bag that math book.

You need money for a book fair at your school's library? How about a few bucks for the guy selling water at the fountains, too? Twenty bucks for a field trip to the art museum? Tell you what: I'll drive you past the Roberto Clemente statue for free.

There's a two-hour delay tomorrow, so Aunt Linda is driving yinz to school. And I'd bundle up if I were you, 'cause they still ain't got no back window.

BOOK-IT

Pizza Hut?! No, I ain't taking you down there. 'Cause you didn't finish none of them Book-Its, that's how's come. The file card on the back of the G.I. Joe figure does *not* count as a Book-It. And no more making up stories. You told your teacher that *The Outsiders* was about a pony that could stay out all night. Last time you just did Book-Its on your Nintendo instructions: "How to Kill Bowser." Other kids were doing *Catcher in the Rye*, you were writing "How to Get to Rainbow Road" on Mario Kart. And don't think that them Choose Your Own Adventures count as five books. I'm on to that scam.

PARENT/TEACHER CONFERENCE

Is this Brandon's class? How's about we get this parent/teacher conference up and flying so's I can get home before the puck is dropping? Tell me everything he's doing wrong so's I know how loud to yell when I get home.

He got an N in Spelling? *That* bad?! I didn't even know it went past F. Maybe he ain't the only one here that needs help spelling. Oh, N is for "needs improvement." Well, it says here he spelled "flower" "F-L-A-H-R." And he keeps putting an *r* in "warsh." I don't know where he's getting that from.

"The sweeper needs fixed." What's wrong with that? Sounds right. Well, at least he got a K in gym. Is that for "kickball"? What the hell is a W for? I can't decipher any of this. Well, how's he gonna understand this if I can't understand this? Well, when he gets home, he's gonna get another N . . . for "No more Nintendo." I'm gonna hook him on phonics . . . with a lock and chain.

Let's talk about extra credit. You got gutters you need cleaned out? Sounds to me like you're gonna need him for some summer school. All summer. The one where they sleep over, too; do that one.

It's a shame yinz don't give out grades for Minecraft. We'd finally have a valedictorian on our hands.

Says he "couldn't remember the 'States' Names' song." Got all that memory used up on what order to beat all the Mega Man bad guys. There ain't no room left for states.

No, he didn't bring home his workbook. The only thing he remembers to bring home from school is strep throat and the stomach flu. And I wanna know where all his jackets are going. We send him here with one, he comes back with nothing. You'd think yinz were starting your own Burlington's Coat Factory in here.

And quit sending my kids home with all this candy to sell, 'cause they don't sell none of it! They just eat it all and tell me I owe the school forty dollars. At least have them sell something I can use. Like fishing lures or beer cozies.

Every time I turn around this school nails me for twenty dollars. "How does *Charlotte's Web* end? Go get twenty dollars off your old man and we'll tell ya!" Paid for that field trip to the science center and he spent all his birthday money on astronaut ice cream. Take them somewhere free, like down the dairy. Or down the crick and lift up a rock. Boom. Science.

Brandon used a cuss word? Where'd he hear that?! It was a rough Steelers season.

You got Jeffy in your class, too? Boy, you're earning your money. Way tougher than when Michelle Pfeiffer tried to teach Coolio. I'm surprised any of your markers still write. That kid sniffs Sharpies dry. Jeffy's in the gifted program?! Gifted at what, eating grasshoppers?

Maybe I oughtta come down and teach some classes. First lesson: how to go through the Sunday paper without tearing it all up!

STREETLIGHTS

What do you mean you didn't know it was time to come in? The streetlights are on! I know Jeffy's allowed to stay out late. His dad's an idiot. He buys batteries down 7-Eleven!

And where are your tennis shoes? Your feet are all black. You look like a damn Vietnam POW. You lost your shoes down the crick?! Everything ends up down the crick. I should just start sending my paycheck down the crick. Were them your good school shoes? Well, looks like you're wearing a pair of your sister's shoes to school tomorrow.

I see your bike is laying in the driveway. Yeah, you'll remember to move it after it's under my car.

What are all these jars of mud water? Magic potions?! Yinz weren't drinking them were ya? The only "magic" they got is teleporting you to the emergency room.

No, your opportunity for a bedtime snack has come and gone. Better luck tomorrow.

Can you stay up late to watch *The Daily Show*?! You're eight years old; you can read *The Huffington Post* tomorrow, Mr. Brokaw.

You got to the count of ten to get inside and get in the tub. One . . . two . . . *NOW*!

WATCHING THE PITTSBURGH STEELERS

It's time for my weekly heart attack, otherwise known as watching the Pittsburgh Steelers.

I'm sorry, Deb, but the TV room is gonna be rated R for the next hour. On the bright side, the swear jar can now put the kids through college. Community college at least.

I tell ya, the league wants the Steelers to lose! Goodell sits around all off-season and figures out new ways to screw us. I'm surprised he even lets us know what time our games are.

Get rid of that stupid instant replay! It slows the pace of the game down. At this rate, it's gonna end up being Tuesday Morning Football. This game has got too much technology nowadays. I'm surprised they don't got Terminators playing by now.

Are they just gonna kick field goals all day?! Geez, all this damn kicking, I thought I accidentally changed the channel to *Bend It Like Beckham*.

Deb, how's come you got to ask me so many questions during the game? I don't know how long Big Ben and his wife have been married, how many kids they got, or if he gets a chance to talk to her at half time. All I know is the score is tied.

No, Linda, we ain't "checking in" on *Dancing with the Stars*! Touch that remote and you're gonna be *seeing* stars.

That missed field goal is all my fault. I have to be kneeling behind the couch for the Steelers to make long field goals.

Well, Deb, when I ain't around to see the grandkids, you can blame it on the ten years this game just shaved off my life.

NFL REFS

What the hell's the ref doing under that hood so long, checking Facebook? Well, your status says "idiot." Oh, he's gotta call upstairs. The way every call is going against us, who's answering . . . Ray Lewis?

NFL ANNOUNCERS

What do you know about anything, Phil Simms?! Why don't you announce games for teams that actually want you: the Giants. The end.

How's come they got Skeletor announcing the game? *That's* Cris Collinsworth?! I'm turning the sound off on the TV and listening to the radio.

THE BALTIMORE RAVENS

The Steelers are named after the hardworking men of the steel industry. The Ravens are named after a poem. Who's their offensive coordinator, Robert Frost?

The only way the Ravens will beat the Steelers is if that Bane from *Batman* shows up and blows up the field. Heck, we still scored even when he did that.

You know what could help yinz out? If you had more purple in your jerseys. That's a man's color. 'Cause when I think football, I think purple. Tom's wife got so much Ravens purple on, my kids thought she was Grimace. They ran up to her begging for chicken nuggets. Even weirder is, she had some! You can cover them in as much purple as you want, we all know they're still just the Cleveland Browns.

There's a Baltimore Raven on *Dancing with the Stars*? What song is he dancing to, "Jailhouse Rock"?

Hey, Tom, if you're gonna theme your house with all that Ravens crap, then you better put some bars on the windows, too!

Tom, I win that Powerball and I'll buy you Ravens season tickets. 'Course, I'll also buy the team and have them moved to the WNBA.

If the Ravens win, I bet they take a bunch of shots after the game. Mug shots!

Aw, I know we ended your fifteen-game home-win streak yinz had. But yinz still got that other streak going: losing in the playoffs.

Everyone in Baltimore keeps blabbing about Torrey Smith? What's the other receiver's name, Becky?

Nobody wants to be in Baltimore. Even the Colts had enough sense to get the hell outta there.

RAY LEWIS

Too bad Ray Lewis ain't ten years younger, he may have been able to stop us. Then again, he might be in jail. He was just fuming on that sideline. Looked like he could kill somebody.

Geez, the way these announcers keep talking up that Ray Lewis, you'd think he brought down the Berlin Wall, ended apartheid, and caught bin Laden.

When is Ray Lewis gonna knock it off with that dance of his? Seen him dancing so much I half expect him to show up at my daughter's tap recital. And why's Ray Lewis always crying? Like he watched *The Notebook* before he come out onto the field.

Don't worry, Tom, you'll still get to see Ray Lewis on television after he retires. In an episode of *COPS*.

JOE FLACCO

Ain't no one in the world give the Steelers a chance to win 'cause we started a third-string quarterback. Of course, with Joe Flacco, yinz start a third-string quarterback every game. Flacco looks like he never knows what's going on. Every time he comes on the field, it's like he just got woken up from a deep sleep. And old James Harrison is right there to put him back in it!

Flacco's eyebrow is way outta control. Heck, it got credited with a third down conversion.

THE CLEVELAND BROWNS

My kids trade their Little Debbie snacks for better stuff than the Cleveland Browns.

I seen players get drafted to the Browns say, "No thanks," and go work down the grocery store.

Beating Cleveland is like resealing the driveway. It's easy and you gotta do it at least once a year.

TOM BRADY

Who am I rooting for? Whoever takes out Tom Brady. I bet you that Gisele ain't even rooting for him. Only person rooting for Tom Brady is Phil Simms. The way he talks about him, you'd think they were going to prom together.

I bet you they fine James Harrison just for watching Tom Brady get sacked.

PEYTON MANNING

Peyton Manning snaps his neck off, comes back and throws fifty-five touchdown passes. My brother-in-law sprains his knee, ain't worked steady for two years.

Geez, what is Peyton Manning now, sixty-eight? Sitting on the sidelines watching *Murder She Wrote*. He's so old, you can probably play as him in that Nintendo Tecmo Bowl game. Try to play as him and the game says, "Are you sure? You know we got Joe Montana on here, right? You want to pick Emmitt Smith and see how he throws the ball maybe?"

Peyton Manning always supports that pizza chain, Pap Pap Johns. I ordered from that place, but the kid wouldn't take my coupon because I "didn't really have one." I'll never order from there again.

TROY POLAMALU

All these players yelling and screaming after they win. Calm down. After Troy Polamalu wins, he paints a landscape, prays, then goes to bed early.

NFL COACHES

Bill Belichick looks like he just pulled his clothes out of the hamper.

Why's that Giants coach Tom Coughlin always look like he's windburned? Only coach I know that could hit the Powerball and still look like a grumpy old tree.

I ain't even seen my own kids throw temper tantrums like them Harbaugh brothers. You'd have thought Daddy Harbaugh just told 'em they can't go in the McDonald's ball pit. Only way the refs get them to behave is by threatening to take away their Nintendo.

Does that Jim Harbaugh even own any other pants besides khakis? I swear, you look at his wedding photo . . . khakis. Sled riding . . . khakis. Swimming in the ocean down Myrtle Beach . . . khakis.

Old John Elway with them teeth. Nowadays, he looks like a horse that sipped out of the wrong Holy Grail.

SEATTLE

Seattle ain't no football town. It's practically Canada. The only thing that come out of Seattle is rain, twelve-dollar coffee, and Nirvana. Outta Pittsburgh you got steel, ketchup, and the mum from *The Partridge Family*.

Seattle Seahawks always bragging about that twelfth man, all loud. Back in the day, Mean Joe Greene would tell the crowd down Three Rivers to shut the hell up so's he could hear the quarterback's bones snap during his hits.

AT YOUR FIRST NFL FOOTBALL GAME

I should be filming you at your first game, Brandon, but I'm sure Bill Belichick got a camera in here somewhere, so we'll just ask him for a copy.

I remember the first time your pap took me to a game. That was a great day. Until the other team kicked a game-winning field goal and we weren't allowed to talk the whole way home.

No, pal, I ain't gonna sit down. You stand up! Where you think you are, Carnegie Hall? You think we came here to see *Wicked* or something? We ain't watching *Less Miserables*. You're making me *more* miserable.

Cover your ears, Brandon. I don't want you to have to hear what I'm gonna yell.

Don't be afraid to hug another man in the stadium. We're all family in here. Perfectly acceptable. I've hugged plenty of men in here after we won. Even been invited to a couple Thanksgivings.

No, I ain't paying to bring your mum down to a game so she can just sit and play Words with Friends. Like this guy doing a crossword puzzle. Give your ticket to someone who cares! What's a three-letter word for idiot? You!

I like being at the game 'cause you can see what you want to see, not what the TV says you have to see. The TV would never let you see Joe Flacco crying down there on the sideline like that. You can tell it's Flacco from all the way up here. Just one big eyebrow.

THE THERMOSTAT

Deb, what do you mean the heat is on? You better be talking about that *Beverly Hills Cop* song!

I thought I smelled heat. You know we don't turn the heat on until after Thanksgiving. Heat is for company.

Yinz are cold? Then let me just turn that thermostat all the way up to "raking leaves." That'll warm ya up! If you're cold, put on a sweater. Or go lay with the dog.

Seventy-five degrees?! You trying to make it a sauna in here? I didn't even put the plastic on the windows yet. Most of that heat is going right out! And look at yinz, all walking around barefoot in shorts and T-shirts like it's a Sandals resort. You're too cold now; next you'll be too hot and running the air-conditioning.

I got this thermostat all programmed and yinz are tapping buttons like you're trying to get back up in Mike Tyson's Punch-Out!!

Heat in October or Christmas presents in December. It's your choice.

I don't care if Linda, Rick, and the kids are coming over.

Rick ain't even fixed the back window of his car yet. He got grocery bags and duct tape covering it up.

No, we ain't getting a frost tonight. Weather guys just say that. Probably getting kickbacks from the power company.

You're gonna move to a hotel? Well, then just try to get comfortable thinking about that *Dateline* special about what they found in them beds.

OK, I'm setting the thermostat on 66 for Mario Lemieux. It goes back up to Mean Joe Greene again, and we got problems.

SHOPPING AT IKEA

This is the only store I know where you buy a lounge chair, wrapping paper, batteries, and meatballs.

You goofs realize you're trying to turn on a fake TV, right? How's that working out for ya? Jeffy! That ain't a real toilet! Put your pants back on.

Yeah, Deb, I sent Jeffy over to the play area. They sent him back. That kid's been red-flagged like that monkey in *Outbreak*. They got his picture up on play areas all over town. "Don't let this kid in the ball pit."

What do you want, Jessica? A little play kitchen? So you can fill that up with dirty dishes, too? Why would I get you a pretend kitchen when you don't do nothing in the real one? I'm about to get you a job working in IKEA's kitchen.

Jessica, you got enough stuffed animals. You're like the Sarah McLachlan of stuffed animals.

We're in a nice store; you don't act like that! You save that behavior for school. 'Cause I ain't there.

Just pretend this whole store is one giant "good living room" and don't touch nothing.

Nah, Mandy, you ain't getting a futon. I don't want you and your boyfriend sitting on nothing that turns into a bed.

Geez, I dunno where I'm at. I swear, this place is a giant maze. I half expect to see David Bowie chasing Jennifer Connelly on the ceiling. Turn the corner and find a frozen Jack Nicholson. We came past this living room three times already. It's like a *Scooby-Doo* background. Oh, you're supposed to follow the glowing arrows. Like when you stand around too long in Double Dragon.

What are yinz doing up there? You was following the arrow?! Ain't no arrows pointing up to the couches hanging on the wall. Get offa that!

No, we ain't playing The Floor Is Lava in the mattress department. How's about we play The Store Is a Jagger Bush and you don't touch nothing. Or yinz can go home and play Your Bedroom Is Jail.

BUILDING FURNITURE

All right, it's that time of year, everybody outta the house. Dad has to build something. It's the same rules as when I'm doing taxes or it's Shark Week. It's easy. It's like building LEGOs. Only I ain't gonna step on this at three in the morning or suck it up into the sweeper. No, Brandon, it ain't like building Minecraft. After I'm done with this, I've actually done something with my life.

Now, what do I need to build this? Just an Allen wrench? That's it? Geeze, just to build that little artist's easel of yours, I needed a table saw, a chalk line, a winch, cobblestones, a Horcrux, something borrowed, something blue.

How's come the instructions ain't got no words? Oh, you just gotta follow the pictures like it's a *Ziggy* comic. Who's gonna show me how to put together the end table, *Beetle Bailey*? *Doonesbury* gonna build the bookcase?

Hey, Deb, grab my boombox, will ya. I wanna listen to music while I build. It's outta batteries? Then just grab Teddy Ruxpin. Works just the same. Plus, you get to hear Steve Perry coming outta Teddy's mouth.

No, Deb, I don't want Uncle Rick's help. That guy put together Barbie's Dream House and it went up in flames. Barbie took a ride on the elevator . . . it was her last ride. They still ain't found Ken.

Deb, this is *your* dresser for more of *your* clothes. All my stuff could fit in the box this dresser came in, for crying out loud. No, don't throw the box out. The kids are getting that for Christmas.

I don't know what this is I just screwed on here. Part of Castle Grayskull? Well, it's part of the dresser now. He-Man's just gonna have to keep his sword in Mum's dresser now.

No, Deb, that bookcase ain't for them creepy, faceless Willow Tree people. None of that. This is to display my chunk of AstroTurf from Three Rivers, the Long John Silver's holiday crystal, and the Dean Martin Roast DVDs.

My grandma never had a piece of furniture in her house that wasn't cedar. Always worried about moths. Her biggest fears in life were moths and black ice.

There, done. Look at how nice that looks. Aw, great. We got extra pieces. What am I supposed to do with these? Just put 'em where we put everything else . . . in the Monopoly game. We need something to replace the iron, anyhows.

HOME DECORATING

Deb, what is it with you decorating the house with spaghetti in jars? What's next, you gonna put a pizza in a picture frame?

What do you think about putting up a big mirror behind

our bar? It'll make it look like there's a whole other room back there. Until your idiot sister tries walking into it like a bird.

DECORATING YOUR BEDROOM

Are these posters of yours stuck in the wall with thumbtacks?! I told yinz to use poster mounts! Boy, you kids must never want me to be able to resell this house. And look at that Miley Cyrus poster. That's scarier than anything you see on TV. That whole wall is gonna have STDs. My homeowners insurance don't cover biohazards.

Did you print out these pictures on your wall with the inkjet?! Must have used a whole cartridge on New Kids on the Block and Fred Savage! Well, guess what you're getting for Christmas? New ink cartridges.

LEAVING THE LIGHTS ON

It costs me a nickel every time you kids turn a light on. This is why we keep getting thank-you cards from the power company.

Why's the Xbox on, ain't nobody playing it? What do you mean it's in "sleep mode"? It's gonna be in "garbage mode" if you don't shut it off.

Whaddya mean it's an "energy-saving bulb"? You know what saves more energy? Shutting it off.

LIGHTS-OUT

Yinz want to buy a lantern? Keep leaving the lights on in the house and that's all you'll be using. Like Abe Lincoln. He turned out all right. What'd he do?! Let me see, five-dollar bill. Statue down Washington. Spielberg movie. Geez, what's that school teaching yinz?

POWER OUTAGES

Aw, Deb, whaddya mean Yankee Candles are "too nice" for a power outage?! Lights are out, I'm burnin' the Meadow Showers.

Nobody open the fridge. I don't want the milk to go bad.

Deb, I'm not screwing with the clock radio right now. Just subtract an hour till we spring ahead again.

THE REFRIGERATOR

Who left the fridge open? Are we using the refrigerator as an air conditioner now? That motor will keep running and then it's ruined! Then we're down to only two fridges in the house. Plus the freezer in the garage.

And quit holding the door open while you're looking. You're letting all the cold air out. You think about what you want, and then you open the door.

Yinz ate all my Klondikes? I tell ya, all you kids do is eat. What, are your legs hollow? I'm one step ahead of you. I hid a good Crunch Klondike in here behind the broccoli so . . . *AW, YOU GOT THAT ONE TOO?!*

Deb, what's this frozen hunk of foil in the freezer? Our wedding cake?! What for? Good luck?! Well, all the Klondikes are gone, so I don't think it's working.

How do I know this frozen dinner ain't no good? Well, for starters it's got coupons for Rax on the box.

Who drank all the iced tea and then put the empty carton back in the fridge? You're "saving it for a bird house"? Bad enough I gotta pay for you kids, now I'm taking care of the neighborhood birds?

This itty-bitty thing of mustard don't go on the big top shelf. That's prime real estate up there. Mustard is a door item.

Deb, I don't care what you saw on *Rachael Rays*, *Ellen*, or *Alive with Regis and Kelly Lee*, stop putting the bread in the fridge. Those people get paid to just talk even though they don't know nothing about anything. If they told you to start washing your face with motor oil, you'd do it.

The milk is fine. Yinz act like it turns into Ebola the second it hits its expiration date.

Who opened a new bottle of ketchup? There's a bunch of perfectly good McDonald's ketchup packets in the junk drawer. Use them first.

Can we take down some of the stuff off this fridge, or do we really need to remember what the middle school was serving for lunch in May 2009?

CRAFT BEERS

No, I don't need a pumpkin-flavored beer. How's about a *beer*-flavored beer?

EATING CEREAL

Did yinz open a new box of cereal before finishing the first one? The Golden Grahams are gone already?! Boy, I can't wait till you kids grow up and have to buy your own cereal. Then you'll see how expensive it is. And quit sticking your hand down in the cereal box to get the toy. All the boxes are bulging out.

You better drink that milk. There's half a gallon sitting in that bowl. This is two bucks' worth of milk I'm supposed to just dump down the sink?

No, I ain't driving to get more milk for your cereal. Just use half and half. Or water. Works just the same.

Don't throw them Corn Pops out. You just mix what's left with the Lucky Charms and Cocoa Krispies. It's like a cereal salad.

Now you're putting sugar on your Frosted Flakes?! I might as well save you the trouble, take ya down the garage, and just saw your foot off right now, Wilford Brimley.

SNACKS

You put a bag of popcorn in there for fifteen minutes?! It's Orville Redenbacher, not Stephen King's *Firestarter*.

Oh, hot damn, I actually found some potato chips in this bag of air I bought.

CHOOSING A RESTAURANT

Will the kids like that restaurant?! I dunno, they have really strict criteria. Do they serve chicken fingers and is there a "play place" attached to it?

AT A RESTAURANT

No, we're sitting at a booth, 'cause I want you kids all squished together on one side. The less you can move, the better. Booths are like milk and bread before a snowstorm . . . they go fast.

Linda, the hostess ain't gonna seat us way back there 'cause there is no "way back there." You're looking at a mirror. You didn't notice your twin pointing back at you?

Quit fighting about crayons! This look like art class? Got all them crayons at home you just leave lying around for the dog to eat, but the second we get out to eat, yinz is hoarding and trading 'em like they was stocks and bonds. Boy, when there's no toys around it don't take you kids ten minutes before you turn into *Lord of the Flies*.

I don't want anything at the table with an On/Off switch. Wish you kids came with an On/Off switch!

ORDERING FOOD

I should be allowed to order off the senior menu after all the gray hair you kids have given me.

No, Brandon, you ain't ordering nothing for dinner that includes the words "cookie," "fudge," or "fantasy." We're ordering real food now. And no, you ain't ordering cereal; we got that at home. If you order an adult-size burger you better be able to finish an adult-size burger. Your eyes are bigger than your stomach.

"Breakfast Smile," "Waffle Smile," "Griddle Smile" . . . How's about I just order the breakfast pieces I want and the waitress will figure out what kinda "smile" it is?

Dad, just order a lemonade. No more of that ordering water, lemon wedges, and Sweet'N Low to mix your own Mr. Wizard drink.

What do you mean I can't have fries 'cause you're getting them, Deb? No, we ain't doing that tag-team dinner thing no more. Just 'cause I'm sharing my life with you don't mean I got to share my Super Burger, too.

No, Brandon, I ain't paying for you to add the salad bar just so you can eat a whole plate of Jell-O. Mum can bring you some croutons from her trip.

KNOWING WHEN TO LEAVE

Two more bites and you can have a dessert. It's one more bite just to get a ride home.

Where yinz going? Nah, that salad bar is all-day. If we stick around until we get hungry, we can hit it up again.

TRAFFIC

You got four seasons in this town: winter, more winter, traffic, and stinkbugs.

They don't even bother putting up detour signs anymore. It just says GOOD LUCK!

Geez, who the hell needs that Governor Christie to cause a traffic jam? All ya need is a tunnel.

THE DEPARTMENT OF TRANSPORTATION

PennDOT is just like a groundhog. They stand around staring for a bit, make as many annoying holes as they can, then go to sleep all winter.

PennDOT ain't fixing them potholes. They're just waiting for the rest of the city to sink down eight inches.

You don't need Bane to shut Gotham City down. You can just send PennDOT in.

They're working on Route 51 now? Well, looks like you kids ain't gonna see your grandma for a couple months. You're just gonna have to FaceTime her.

"Fresh Oil and Chips"? More like New Dings and Dents!

Ain't no way I'm stopping at that store. It ain't on our side of the road.

PROPER DRIVING

Look at this goofball kid driving with his seat reclined all the way back. Looks like he's driving in a dentist's chair.

GIVING DIRECTIONS

Where you trying to get to? What you're gonna do is go down through three stop signs. Once you get to that third stop sign . . . go through that stop sign. You're gonna come to a house with a big lava rock in the front yard. You make a right there. But if you reach the ball fields, you gone too far. You're gonna turn left at the insurance agency that they made out of an old Pizza Hut. But if you pass the Pizza Hut they turned into a day-care center, you gone too far. Go past that road stand where they sell that good sweet corn.

Hey, Deb, is that the Blue Belt or the Green Belt? Whaddya mean it's by Sue's house?! He don't know Sue! Ain't no road sign say THIS WAY TO SUE'S HOUSE.

No, it's Moon *Township*, Deb! You think I got Neil Armstrong asking for directions here?

You're gonna go through the tunnel and everyone is gonna slow down for no reason.

Nowadays, five o'clock traffic starts at two. Hey, Deb, is there a Penguins game tonight? Oh, don't go down that way then. You know what? You're better off just going back home.

HALLOWEEN

Sure, I'll take yinz down to the Halloween store. It's called Goodwill.

I don't care if you are Batman, you're eight years old and it's fifty degrees outside; you're wearing a winter jacket!

Mandy, what are you wearing?! That ain't a cat! Go up and put more fur on! Cats ain't sexy, they're annoying. How 'bout you go as a "sexy janitor" and you can start by taking out the kitty litter. You go to a party as "Sexy Cat" and you're gonna see me show up as "Enraged Father."

You don't need a new glow stick. There's still one sitting in the freezer from last year.

Trick-or-treating is starting already? Ain't even dark yet! The news ain't even on yet. I want you kids back here ten minutes after the fire whistle goes off. Not sitting down on the corner trading candy. And don't just go biting into them Reese's Cups till I check 'em for needles and glass. I gotta taste everything to see if it's safe.

You kids look too old to be trick-or-treating. How do I know?! Well, for starters, you pulled up in a car.

Sure, Deb, next year we can give out full-size candy bars. Along with the deed to the house. Why don't we just let kids walk through the house and pick out what they want like it's *Wheel of Fortune*?

We're all out of candy? Well, grab them Halls eucalyptus cough drops up on my nightstand.

Watch out for that bumblebee kid. He been here three times already.

How long does Halloween go on tonight? I tell ya, after this I'm going trick-or-treating down the beer distributor.

TELLING SCARY STORIES

The only scary story I can tell you is the "Tale of the 2003 Steelers." They went six and ten. It was terrifying.

IT'S BEDTIME

What's this I hear about you won't go to sleep? You're scared
of zombies?! You was watching *The Walking Dead* again after
your mum told you not to! Don't worry, zombies are slower
than hell. They're like old people in the self-checkout line at
the grocery store. You'll have plenty of time to get away. Even
if you did get bit by a zombie, your mum got plenty of Bac-
tine. That works for everything. Bee stings. Jagger pricks.
Zombies.

When you close your eyes, don't think about zombies. Think about rainbows and kitty cats and marrying that *Twilight* Mexican werewolf kid you like. Oh, you're done with him? You're on to that *Hungry Games* kid now?

No, you can't sleep with Mum and me. Dr. Phil said it ain't good . . . for your math-skills development or something. You wanna sleep with the dog? That lazy thing wouldn't even notice if a zombie took a bite out of him.

Board up the windows?! You want boarded-up windows, go live in Cleveland.

THINGS THAT GO BUMP IN THE NIGHT

What do you mean Aunt Linda seen a ghost?! She also "saw" Alan Thicke down Fantastic Sam's, so I wouldn't put too much stock in what she says.

Deb, there's not a burglar downstairs, it's one of the kids. Burglars usually don't make microwave popcorn before they rob you.

A ZOMBIE INVASION

Zombies?! We'll be fine. Got about a hundred TV dinners downstairs and Brandon got that ninja sword from the flea market.

Don't even bother barricading the house, 'cause Jeffy from down the street would *still* find a way to get in. Other day I seen him down a storm drain "looking for the Ninjer Turtles." I said I hope he finds the clown from *IT*. Then again the clown from *IT* is probably afraid of running into Jeffy. Jeffy knows the clown from *IT*'s fears.

When the zombies come, we'll need the good camping equipment. What do you mean you left it down Rzepniak's house?! Well, that's gone. Probably traded it for a case of beer by now.

No, we ain't going to hole up at the mall. I'll be fighting off zombies, Deb will be trying out Bath & Body Works lotions.

Get a helicopter?! Who the hell's gonna fly it, Linda, you? Back in high school you derailed the Christmas train down the mall. Kids was jumping off like it was *The Fugitive*. The guy from KayBee Toys had to hand out blankets. Had a candlelight vigil at Wicks 'N' Sticks. The piano and organ store played nothing but hymns.

Deb, you're gonna kill zombies?! You freak out when a stinkbug lands in your hair. You make me get a paper towel and flush it down the toilet.

My ultimate zombie team would be: Snake Eyes from G.I. Joe, Stone Cold Steve Austin, and Pat Morita . . . if he were still alive. But he could come back as a zombie, so I'd probably keep him on the team anyways. Can you imagine if a zombie Pat Morita come out?

Yes, Jessica, we're still going to church during the zombie apocalypse. Probably even more often. And CCD, you ain't getting outta that, either.

VETERANS' DAY

My grandfather invaded Germany. Pap fought the Vietcong. But of course you kids wanna skip a Veterans' Day service to jerk around at the mall.

Deb, I hung that pole so we could hang a flag for Veterans' Day, not so you could put up a Christmas flag two weeks before Thanksgiving.

WATCHING TV

You girls have to watch cheerleading somewhere else 'cause your brother and I are watching wrestling on the big TV.

How's come every time you kids is done playing video games, my TV don't work? And quit taking the batteries outta the remotes to put in your Game Boy. You better hope I got more double A's in the freezer.

We got one TV and about seven remotes. What do all these do?!

"DVR full"?! How many *CSI*s you taping, Deb?

Why's everybody's faces all stretched out? Now what are those black bars on the top and bottom? I didn't pay for that big TV to see half a screen! No, I don't need to read what everyone is saying.

No, Deb, you can't use aluminum foil on a flat screen. That don't work no more.

Who's this old lady shrieking on the TV? That's Steven Tyler?! Poor guy sounds like an old hunting dog caught up in jagger bushes. Geez, in that leather jacket, he looks like one of them aged Sioux Indian chiefs.

Only person on that *Walking Dead* show that's worth anything is Daryl. They should make a whole show about Daryl. You can cut out that "Tracy Chapman with a sword" girl. "Wilford Brimley on one leg"? Cut him out.

Aw, Deb, the kids deleted one of your *True Blood*s. You're just gonna have to get your Joe . . . Mango-Jello fix some other way this week.

What else did you kids tape? *Nightmare Before Christmas*?! Aw, when Mum finds out, we're about to *live* the Nightmare Before Christmas.

If there were a real Sharknado, the Pittsburgh weathermen woulda just called it "partly cloudy" and still sent you kids to school.

Mandy, we ain't watching no show called *16 and Pregnant*! How's 'bout finding a show called *18 and Gone*?

Hey, I just sent *Grown Ups 2* back to Netflix, yet I see the *Grown Ups 2* disc here on the floor. What the hell was in that envelope, then?

What, Linda? What's our HBO GO password?! If you wanna watch *Game of Thrones*, you can HBO *go* pay your own damn cable bill.

Will I watch *The Biggest Loser* with you? Oh, is Tom trying to parallel-park his car again?

Nah, Deb, you know when *Shawshank's Redemption* is on TV, Dad's done for the day.

What are you squealing about? A *Boy Meets World* sequel?! How's about *Girl Meets Dishes*? Get going.

AT THE VIDEO STORE

All right, yinz can pick out one video each. Not that Chipmunk movie again. Get something yinz ain't seen yet. I ain't paying for a video that yinz can recite line for line.

Deb, how about that new one with Adam Sanders and *The King of Kings* guy we like? Is that out yet?

No, I ain't sitting through another *Sex with the City* movie and watching four women yap about shoes for two hours.

We should get some old *Three Stooges*; they're funny. Aw, Deb, what do you know about comedy? You laugh at that Kathy Griffins.

No, you kids can't watch that movie. There's naked sex in that. PG rating or under.

Deb, see if that guy coming in the store right now is bringing back *The Bucket List*.

Here's the movie, but it says "Blu-ray" on it. It's the same movie, I don't care what color the disc is. What do you mean we need a whole other machine to play it?! I bet it plays in my DVD player just the same. They're just trying to hose you into buying something new that you don't really need.

No, I ain't watching *The Notebook* with you, Deb. Last time you watched that, you were crying like one of the kids died.

Uncle Rick ain't allowed to rent videos from nowheres

anymore. He always left tapes in the hot car. He's melted just about every movie from *Alien* all the way to *Zoolander*.

Do I want to rewatch *Titanic*?! I'm sorry, but I have to get to work by Monday.

I said yinz could rent a movie, not a video game. Those are two dollars more. Unless you want to spend your birthday money?

If you can't decide on a movie soon I'm going to grab the first movie I see that starts with a *W* and ends with "*-ild Hogs*."

Quit running around in here; this ain't a gym! And where'd yinz get all that candy? Did yinz run into Willy Wonka, or what? Put it all back. We got popcorn at home.

What do you mean there's a fifteen-dollar late fee on our card? You had that Facebook movie out so long we could've bought it!

No, yinz ain't getting another *Chucky* movie. Last time yinz watched one of them, you all had to sleep in Mum and me's bed for a week. I had to put all your dolls up in the shed.

Deb, check that Redbox to see if they got that new movie with Tom Hanks fighting them pirates on that cruise ship.

Deb, this movie looks good. It's got a little green guy coming out of the toilet on the box.

All right, I got a nice family movie for us to watch. *The Terminator*.

DISNEY MOVIES

It's a Disney movie, so the parents made it a whole ten minutes before dying on a boat. If you're a parent in a Disney movie, you ain't making it to the end credits. Them Disney parents should know better by now. Don't go on no trips. Don't get remarried. Don't stay in an old castle when it's raining out. And don't be a deer. Everyone always wondered in *Toy Story* where Andy's dad was. He saw that Disney logo and was outta there before that little lamp even came bouncing out. Now he's just paying child support and living with a younger woman he met down Chipotle.

DISNEY'S *FROZEN*

Everybody is trying to figure out how to stop this Ice Queen. I says just dump a bag of rock salt on her. Movie over. Use that good Driveway Heat.

She runs off to the mountains and every li'l girl and mum in the place starts singing "Let it go. . . Let it go . . ." I says "Let *me* go. . . see *Robocop*."

They got a talking snowman in this. Can you imagine if that snowman in Tom's yard start talking? Yeah, the one with a corncob pipe and dog-crap eyes. That snowman would be begging someone for a hair dryer so he could melt himself down, put himself out of his misery.

And the one sister is so cold she's turning into ice. I says just cut open that reindeer like a Tauntaun and shove her in there. But she ends up turning into an ice sculpture, like that one the guy with a chainsaw made down the work Christmas party where you could drink Yuengling outta the Stanley Cup.

Now my girls been playing that soundtrack on repeat for two months. So I "let it go." Out the window.

THE LEGO MOVIE

Can we get *The LEGO Movie*?! You kids got LEGOs. Get outside and make your own movie.

Boy, LEGO got me with this one. Got *me* to pay twenty dollars so you kids could watch a two-hour commercial five times a day. You know where else you can watch commercials? On TV. For free. "Everything Is Awesome"? They should be singing "Everything's Expensive."

Well, how's *The LEGO Movie* end? They all get sucked up into the sweeper?

See, the movie's telling you to use your imagination. So just imagine you actually own some LEGOs.

Can you imagine if your LEGO guys started talking?

Especially the one the dog ate and then crapped out two days later. I doubt he'd be singing "Everything Is Awesome."

Aw, Batman's in this?! How do you have a Batman with no Michael Keaton voice? That's like having a salad with no french fries on it.

THE HUNGER GAMES

The girls made me take them to see that *Hungry Games* last night. I says, "You want Hungry Games? Sure. I ain't buying no more Go-Gurts."

So, they put all these kids' names in a lottery to see if the kids get taken away. How do I enter that lottery? They got scratch-offs like that down 7-Eleven? Three cherries: "Good luck, Mandy."

My kids wouldn't last five minutes in them games. They nearly starved to death because we was out of Bagel Bites.

TWILIGHT

So, last night Deb and the girls made me watch one of them *Twilight* movies. I never prayed so hard for a stroke in all my life.

This new girl meets this boy and it turns out he's a vampire and he eats people. So I'm thinking, all right, he's a vampire, shouldn't we kill him? Ain't no one gonna throw garlic on anyone? No, she falls in love with him.

Why's this vampire hanging out with teenage girls, anyways? You never saw Grandpa Munster hanging out with teenage girls. Well, not that we know of. He was too busy blowing stuff up in that meth lab in the Munsters' cellar.

No, *Twilight* vampires can go outside during the day. It don't kill them. They just sparkle. I says, "Who ever heard of a twinkly vampire?" I never seen Count Chocula twinkling. His only ability was to rot your teeth.

No, Edward the vampire can't turn into a bat. He hot-rods around town in a little Volvo. 'Cause apparently Dracula is "going green." I kept hoping Smokey and the Bandit would come and run him right off the road.

And the whole time, I'm dozing off. But the girls keep waking me, 'cause apparently, "it gets better."

There's these Indian boys running around and I says, "Where the hell are all their shirts at? Ain't there a JCPenney's in this town?" Then the Indian boys start turning into woofs. I was half expecting the dad to turn into a sexy Frankenstein.

And then the woofs are fighting the vampires over the girl

and Deb turns to me and says, "Are you on Team Edward or Team Jacob?" I says, "How's about Team Normal?!"

They tell me I gotta see the next one 'cause there's a vampire baby. Survey says? WRONG!

MAGIC MIKE

Wait till you hear what movie Deb dragged me to last night. *Mike the Magician.* Wasn't two minutes into the movie and that Channer Tating's walking around with his butt out. I ain't ever seen Siegfried and Roy do that. I thought there'd be card tricks or ladies getting sawed in half. Only thing he made disappear was everybody's pants. What's next? David Copperfield gonna start pole dancing? Penn and Teller giving lap dances? I was just glad that movie wasn't in 3-D.

All the women in the theater are hooting and hollering like they were really at a strip club! I swear a couple of them got pregnant just by watching that movie. And Linda says, "Us girls need to go to that club!" Yeah right, Linda, what are you going to stuff in their pants, Entertainment Book coupons?

One girl was there with her grandma. You're going to give that old woman a heart attack! In her day, guys only wore those full bathing suits like they was circus weightlifters.

Deb says, "Stallone and Schwarzenegger go shirtless in all

their old movies." I says, "Yeah, but they're doing something interesting. Killing guys."

Then, we're leaving the theater and Deb has this look in her eye. Last time I seen that look we ended up with Magic Mandy.

Oh yeah, I'm taking her to see it again tonight. No doubt.

JERSEY SHORE

Hey, something's wrong with the TV; everybody's orange. Aw, what do you mean they're "supposed to look that way?" I didn't know Danny DeVito was on this show. *That's* Snooki?! Well, what the hell's wrong with him?

There's so many bleeps in this show, it's starting to sound like Morse code. I bet you can catch pink eye just from looking at these people.

MUSIC

Miley Cyrus played down Consol Energy Center last night? Then they better just bleach that whole building. That's all we need is Sidney Crosby getting pink eye.

How's come every time Kenny Chesney comes around, you girls look like slutty Lone Rangers? That's barely enough denim to make a pocket!

Yinz have been calling that radio station and you forgot to shut the oven off! The next song you'll be hearing is "Burning Down the House!"

Hey, Jessica, turn down that boy-band music or else you're gonna be heading in "One Direction" . . . your bedroom!

POPULAR LITERATURE

What are you reading, Linda? *Fifty Shades of Grey*?! Don't Rick know nothin' 'bout painting?

WATCHING THE PITTSBURGH PENGUINS

"It's a hockey night in Pittsburgh!" And it's a "homework night" in this house. Get to it.

What channel is the game on anyhows? One night it's on channel 29, the next night it's on NBC. The cable company just loves playing musical chairs with all my programs.

I need everything like 2009, when the Pens last won the Stanley Cup! *Twilight* posters, Uncle Rick in a "Captain Sully" T-shirt, and, Brandon, you in diapers!

Deb, don't sit down. You have to stay standing. The Pens don't score when you sit.

I ain't watching the Pens game at Uncle Rick's tonight. His TV is so old the glow puck still shows up on it.

I'm glad that ol' Geno Malkin escaped Russia. I just hope them Russians don't come over here to try to take him back like it's *Red Dawn*.

Some of the players got less teeth than your pap. No, he didn't play hockey, he just didn't trust fluoride.

3. . . 2. . . 1. . . Win. No, Deb, this game ain't the last one we need to win Lord Stanley. We still got about five more months of playoffs.

SIDNEY CROSBY

Hey, Crosby, be careful! They should just bubble-wrap his whole head. Make him wear his pads and helmet to bed, too. If it were up to me, he would be driving around the city in a child seat.

THE FLYERS

Can't Philadelphia just go away and join a different state already? Ain't nothing good ever come out of that city. Except the Constitution.

It's like God knew that Jaromír Jágr was going to end up playing for the Flyers, because he put "jag" right in his name.

THANKSGIVING

Hey, Deb, what time we eating dinner? Two thirty?! Who the hell eats dinner at two thirty? It gets earlier every year. Next year it'll be Thanksgiving for breakfast.

What time are Linda, Rick, and the kids coming over? I don't even think we got a big enough turkey for that guy. He eats like he's going to the electric chair.

When the kids come in the door, the shoes come off. Every year they come over here, they play a little game I like to call Which One of Us Can Break Something First?

I think we should have three tables this year. We have the adult table, the kids' table, and then my table, which isn't even in the house.

And when Rick starts talking to me about hunting, and I'm not paying attention, I don't wanna hear "What's your problem? Why ain't you talking?" Thanksgiving ain't for talking, it's for football.

No, we ain't watching *Home Alone*. Since when did that become a holiday tradition? Yeah, the Pilgrims and Indians set up their turkey, cornucopia, and then all sat around watching *Home Alone*.

You're out of your mind if you think I'm waiting in line at KMart's at midnight for a toy. There's only one thing I'm doing at midnight. Eating the leftovers.

SHOPPING ON BLACK FRIDAY

I wasn't even halfway through my Thanksgiving Thursday and you're pushing me out the door for Black Friday. The way you shop, Deb, we ain't gonna have any green on Saturday. Look at this store. It's nuttier than the Middle East. People visit the Gaza Strip to get a break from Black Friday. We just had to get down here for the "Doorbusters" sale? The way yinz slam 'em, I got a whole family of doorbusters. All this to save twenty bucks on a sweeper. We don't even need a new sweeper. Unless it comes with some kids that will actually run it.

Why's that guy got a helmet on? I'm getting worried. Any

of these people try pushing me, it's gonna turn out to be a Black-*out* Friday for 'em.

No more layaway, Deb. You had them Cabbage Patch Kids on layaway so long they're Cabbage Patch Adults by now. They didn't come with a birth certificate; they came with Social Security.

How much they selling printers for? Twenty dollars?! That's cheaper than the ink cartridges. Pick up a couple of 'em. We run outta ink, just swap out the whole damn printer.

No, I ain't doing nothing called Cyber Monday. I got the computer blocked against them filth sites.

PLAYING IN THE SNOW

Hey, if you kids are gonna sled ride, you better put grocery bags over your socks. Don't need you catching pneumonia. Then you'll be stuck home from school.

Where's your tossel cap at? I'm surprised you even have gloves on. If it weren't for me and Mum, you'd be sled riding in flip-flops. I don't care if you have a 103-degree fever tomorrow, you're going to school. You're gonna get a nice degree in Get Out of My House.

And if you're sleddin' down at the church, make sure yinz jump off before you hit the road. 'Cause if you come home hurt, don't even bother coming home at all.

Where's your sled? Ain't my fault you left it at the school-yard. Just use a cardboard box; it works just the same. And don't be playing near the house. One of them big icicles is bound to fall off and stab ya in the head. No, don't go and break them off, licking them. They're filthy. You're gonna get diseases.

When you're done playing, you come through the garage, not the front. That's all I need is slushy puddles in the carpets. You know how mad your mum gets whenever her socks are wet. I want you to hang your snow clothes in the utility tub in the basement or on the radiators. And make sure you close the garage door, 'cause I ain't trying to heat the whole neighborhood.

PREPARING FOR THE WORST

Hey, Deb, better run down to the grocery store for milk and toilet paper. The five-day forecast is saying snow tomorrow. We can't wait till tomorrow. By then there'll be bands of warriors on dirt bikes trading body parts for toilet paper.

And check and see if they sell rock salt, too. No, Deb, we only got table salt. What do you expect me to do with that, season the ice? Don't expect the borough to do nothing. They treat rock salt like it was rare diamonds.

And when you're at the store, don't park too close. Park far away. That's all I need is someone ramming a buggy into the side of the car. It's like *Cannonball Run* with buggies down that parking lot. Except there ain't no Burt Reynolds to wink at ya.

Aw, the kids are firing up that Garage Band game again. Better stop at the beer distributor, too.

Another fake snowstorm brought to you by the grocery store's milk and toilet-paper aisles. Do they just call one in when they're overstocked?

SHOVELING SNOW

Geez Louise, at this point if I joined a chain gang I'd be doing *less* shoveling.

No wonder the borough ain't got no salt. You kids tracked it all into the house. I'm surprised there ain't horses in here licking the carpet.

Hey, Tom, you ever think about shoveling that walk of yours? Or throwing some salt down? Or are you trying to set up the *Home Alone* house? And here's another tip: brush some of that snow off the top of your car. It looks like there's a second car just sitting on top of yours.

THE ICE SCRAPER

You took the ice scraper in the house? I should just put the ice scraper in an old Starbucks cup or a Dunkin Donuts bag. That way, it'll never make it outta the car.

THE PARKING CHAIR

Hey, Tom, don't even think about moving this folding chair. I shoveled that spot for my car, not for your old lady. I see your car in that spot and I'm calling Comcast and lettin' them know about you stealin' HBO.

SNOW-DAY SCHOOL CLOSINGS

What the hell are yinz doing up already? School closings?! I should have known. You're hovering around that TV like your mum waiting for the O.J. Simpson verdict.

Oh, you looked away, now they're on the "Saint" schools. Now you gotta wait for the whole thing to come 'round again. Geez, how many Saint schools do they got around here? I think they're just making them up. "St. Ray's of Pitcairn." "St. Donny's Cathedral."

Mandy, you can watch them names go by all you want, but "Pap's Birthday Dinner" ain't gonna scroll by. You're going.

What do you mean there's a Polar Vortex?! That's an American Gladiator. Polar Vortex is just a fancy word for "it's a little chilly out."

Mandy, I doubt your algebra teacher personally called the superintendent pleading with him to keep school open. Them teachers want a day off more than you kids. They're tired of looking at yinz all day.

Yinz got canceled? Sure, scream and cheer now, but don't come crying to me when you're in class during my Fourth of July party. You'll be watching fireworks from the bus stop. Easter vacation, gone. Memorial Day, gone. I'll be opening the pool, you'll be opening books. But you just keep cheering. Live for the day.

No, Jeffy, this house is closed, too! Didn't you see it scroll by on the news? "Brandon's house: CLOSED. No evening activities. No morning K. Now, go away!"

Why don't yinz go shovel driveways for money? And get some practice on ours first.

You left them snow pants in the garage and they froze to the ground. I tried to pick 'em up and they broke apart like the T-1000.

What are you doing now? A snow-cone business?! Well,

you're selling them snow cones for twenty-five cents but using a dollar's worth of juice on each one. Sure glad you got a day off from education.

No, it's way too dangerous to go out on them roads to get a pizza. We'll have one delivered.

I knew school was closed tomorrow when I came home and seen the damn Risk board was out.

We ain't letting this cold go to waste. Let's fill them extra ice-cube trays and put them out on the back porch.

BOREDOM

Hey, yinz can go circle what you want in Penney's Christmas catalog. That's fun. Who said anything 'bout you getting stuff? I'm just talking bout you circling stuff.

CHRISTMAS SHOPPING

OK, I'm giving you each ten dollars to buy Mum something from Santa's Workshop at school. And don't come back here with no hockey-stick pencil toppers, switchblade comb, thumb wrestlers, fake dog crap, ice cubes with a fake fly in it, them sticky whacker

hands, or jars of slime. Mum don't need a camouflage Velcro wallet. You always end up buying something *you* want, then you tell her you'll "show her how to use it," and she don't ever see it again.

No, you can't combine birthdays and future Christmases to get a bigger present this year. What the hell's this look like, Bank of America?

Deb, if you just ordered that gift today, it ain't getting here by tomorrow. It's the mail, not a DeLorean.

ELMO

Jessica, don't tell me you need another Elmo. I've been buying Elmos since 1996. Tickle-Me-Elmo. Hug-Me-Elmo. High-Five-Me-Elmo. I'm waiting for them to make the Elmo that waits in line outside Toys "R" Us to get the next Elmo. Where's Putting-Up-the-Christmas-Lights-Elmo? Or Cutting-the-Grass-Elmo? Or Shoveling-Snow-Elmo? He can laugh the whole time he's doing it.

PLAYING SANTA CLAUS

Hey, Father Tim, this counts as church for me on Sunday. And that collection basket better just pass me up a few times as well.

All right, one at a time you kids can come up. What would you like? An authentic Steelers jersey?! Them's expensive. The elves are trying to get rid of them Santonio Holmes ones, how 'bout that?

What do I smell like? Cigarettes?! Aw, who was wearing this Santa outfit last . . . the Marlboro Man?!

How does Santa get into a house with no chimney?! Well, I'd just push in that old air-conditioning unit your dad leaves in all year and crawl in through the window.

Is it cold up at the North Pole?! Nah, 'cause Mrs. Claus keeps Santa's thermostat set at "Equator."

Yes, you can leave out some of your dog's Beggin' Strips for the reindeer. They won't hurt 'em. Santa's sister-in-law ate those once after she drank too many of her friend Mike's lemonades.

You kids are supposed to be telling me what you want; instead you're putting me on the hot seat asking me all these questions. Watch *The Polar Express* if you wanna know all this stuff. Or Google it.

What do you want? Thundercats?! Well, how's about I just give you *my* cat? There, it's yours, done. Merry Christmas.

You want a new Wii? No, you're getting new tires for your mum's GMC Jimmy. The ones she has are all bald. You'll hit a patch of black ice, flip the car, and end up in a ditch. Merry Christmas.

Hey, Joshua, before you come up here, have Mrs. Claus hit you with a couple pumps of hand sanitizer. Your face is slimier than Jabba the Hutt's. I'm trying to fill stockings this year, not prescriptions.

You want a Transformer? That's it? You're Frank and Pat DeNuzzi's kid, ain't you? Santa's budget for your Christmas could probably get you Michael Bay.

Mandy, let Andrew know that you're to be home by ten o'clock tonight, or else Santa Claus is coming to town . . . with a baseball bat.

OK, Jeffy, c'mon up. Ho, ho, ho, you little jaggo. No, there ain't no way in hell Santa's bringing you any gift that starts with "hydrochloric."

Whaddya want? An Xbox One?! That's five hundred dollars. That's more than Santa's mortgage. Santa already got you the Xbox *None*. It's called the backyard. Wait till you see these graphics; it's like you're really there. Don't you already got an Xbox 360, anyways? Ain't that better? What the hell happened to the other 359 Xboxes? You got that N64 in the garage; that's bigger than one.

What game do you want? Caller Duty: Ghosts?! Well, who do you play as, Patrick Swayze or Whoopi Goldberg? You wanna play with ghosts, we got Pac-Man on the Atari in the basement. There: you got Caller Duty: Ghosts sitting right in your hand! You can't see it?! Well, that means they're doing their job, then.

What game? Rayman Legends?! Who the hell's Raymond? You talking about Ray Ivino? That guy ate a whole Vincent's pizza pie by himself. He *is* a legend.

Easy-Bake Oven?! Just go hold a doughnut up to a lamp; it's the same thing.

Baby Alive Surprise doll?! Yeah, that's what Santa's sister-in-law got when she was sixteen: "baby surprise."

BEING NAUGHTY OR NICE

You kids might not be on Santa's naughty list, but you're sure as hell on mine. You used all your sister's good Proactiv that she gets in the mail to paint your faces like ghosts. You stole Jesus's scepter from the Nativity to play Harry Potter. And you ate the entire month of candy in the advent calendar on the first day. Geez, you kids make me need an Advil calendar.

CHRISTMAS EVE

No, I ain't takin' yinz downtown for Light Up Night. The
house down the street has a bunch of lights; walk down and
look at that.

Deb, there's enough tinsel on the tree! Geez Louise, I can practically see my reflection in it. I don't care if you can see bare spots when you're squinting. Keep it up and you're gonna see a bare spot where the tree used to be.

I told yinz you can open one present when we get back from church. I'm about ready to put barbed wire around that Christmas tree. You kids ask me about presents one more time and I'll call Santa right now and tell him he can just skip this house. "Hello, Santa? I'm calling from Pittsburgh. You can skip this house."

And quit nebbin' up in the attic lookin' for presents! No, Jeffy, that ain't cotton candy lining the roof. Just 'cause something has Pink Panther on it don't mean you start eatin' it. No wonder your throat is itchy. Don't bother lookin' for presents anyhows, 'cause I know where Santa hid 'em. On layaway.

What do you mean you don't wanna watch *Charlie Brown Christmas*?! You kids won't watch nothing unless it's in 3-D and they cast Ryan Gosling as Snoopy and Cedric the Entertainer as the tree.

CHRISTMAS MORNING

I can't get you kids up for school the whole year, but the one day there's a couple wrapped gifts down here, you're like lightning bolts. From now on I'm putting a limit on when you kids can wake up for Christmas morning. It's barely even light out! Next year you'll be down here at twelve-oh-one. I'd hate to be you when Mum comes down and finds you un-wrapped everything already. You better tape all that back up and pretend to be surprised.

CHRISTMAS PRESENTS

Brandon, whaddya mean you "wanted an iPad"? You're eight years old; what are you gonna do with an iPad? Schedule goof-off time with Jeffy? Don't pout, or I'll take back both of them Caller Duty and Hello 4 games.

Mandy, what do you mean "can we exchange it for something else"? You ain't even done unwrapping it. Geez, all you see is the UPC and you already know what it is.

There, you got your skis, your ski boots, your ski jacket, and your ski gloves. Everything you need for the Ski Club. How's about next semester you join the Job Club?

Sorry, Mandy, I didn't know there was that many Jennifer Lopez perfumes. How the hell many different things can one lady smell like anyhows?!

No, Deb, I didn't get you that shower radio. I've been trying to figure out ways to shorten your showers, not extend them!

Which one of yinz already opened Mum's present? Well, it sure as hell wasn't the Elf on the Shelf!

Mandy, get off your phone! I forgot to tell you that Santa don't have an unlimited data plan no more.

How many batteries does that toy horse take? Eight D batteries?! Might as well just go pick up a car battery down Pep Boys! It'd be cheaper to buy yinz a real horse.

Are there any more hidden presents?! Yeah, down in the garage. I got yinz a snow shovel and rock salt. Merry Christmas.

All right, yinz got a few minutes to get ready; we're going to Gram's. Yinz can each bring one toy with ya. No, I don't know what Gram got you. Probably the same things she gets you every year: either one of them coin-wrapping machines or a remote-control car with two foot of wire.

CLEANING UP AFTER CHRISTMAS

I gotta take down these lights in the middle of a blizzard while you kids play your Nintendo DS? There ain't enough beers in a case to deal with this. Well, you might wanna take a few minutes to enjoy these lights, 'cause next Christmas, this house is gonna be dark.

Are we gonna knock these icicles down, or are we hoping Superman moves in?

Hey, Deb, this fake snow crap ain't coming off the windows. You might as well have just used white spray paint. Now I'm gonna have to use the entire tax return on new windows.

And let's redd up all these toys and presents. It's like a North Korean minefield down here with all these LEGOs and Barbie combs.

I got news for that stupid cat laying in the Christmas tree: Your playground's coming down.

How the hell did tinsel make it all the way into the upstairs bathroom? The tree wasn't even near there! Look at this tinsel caught up in the sweeper! I'm gonna have to replace the whole belt.

Aw, who bought the kids Play-Doh? It's all ground up into the carpet! Why can't they be like normal kids and just eat it?

BEING BORED

Don't tell me there ain't nothing to do. This house looks like a damn Toys "R" Us. I'll take all these toys down to Goodwill. How 'bout that? Take you shopping?! Boy, that Christmas money is just burning a hole in your pocket, isn't it?

GETTING SICK

I ain't worried about Ebola. I already survived Jeffy going in the Chuck E. Cheese ball pit. My immune system can beat anything after that.

No, Mandy, I ain't taking you to the emergency room 'cause you got a headache. Go wrap a towel around your head. Your status for school tomorrow got upgraded from "doubtful" to "ain't no way you're taking another sick day 'cause of a head-ache."

Don't touch none of them toys at the doctor's office. They're a trap. They just want you sick so you'll come back. I can't even believe I'm touching this magazine.

NEW YEAR'S EVE

This party is heating up and I ain't even busted out the *Flash-dance* soundtrack yet.

No, no, no, you kids play down the game room. This is an adult party up here, 'cause we're doing adult stuff. So quit nebbing! You got Fireball Island and all them other board games down there, but you keep coming up with excuses to come up here. I only got one game up here for yinz: *Trouble.* And you know what game you'll be playing after that? *Sorry!*

Deb, where's that good mix tape we had with all them Hall & Oates songs? What do you mean it's at your mother's?!

She don't even got a tape deck! She just tried to buy Mandy that Katy Perry album on a record.

Dave, you are not the DJ, 'cause you'll start a song, everyone will get excited, then it always ends up being Weird Al's goofy version.

No, we ain't playing Scattergories. It's a party, not study hall.

OK, kids, the ball is gonna drop! Grab Mum's pots and pans and bang them outside. And not the glass Visions ones like last year!

No, Rick, we ain't shooting off guns. Who do I look like, Yosemite Sam?

STOCKING THE BAR

No, there ain't no wine in this box. Tish ripped the bag out and is carrying it around in her purse like she's a yinzer St. Bernard.

Do we have Zima?! Sure, it's right under here next to the Crystal Pepsi and Slimer's Ecto-Cooler.

GOOD LUCK

No, that stink ain't the dog. That's tomorrow's sauerkraut cooking. Whaddya mean you don't like sauer-

kraut? Sauerkraut is good luck! Everything good that's ever happened to me started with sauerkraut. First date with Deb: sauerkraut. The 2005 Super Bowl: sauerkraut. They built that new Applebee's up the road: sauerkraut.